T0320661

# EFFICIENT PARSING FOR NATURAL LANGUAGE

# THE KLUWER INTERNATIONAL SERIES
# IN ENGINEERING AND COMPUTER SCIENCE

## NATURAL LANGUAGE PROCESSING
## AND MACHINE TRANSLATION

*Consulting Editor*

Jaime Carbonell

# EFFICIENT PARSING FOR NATURAL LANGUAGE

## A FAST ALGORITHM FOR PRACTICAL SYSTEMS

by

**MASARU TOMITA**
Carnegie-Mellon University

**KLUWER ACADEMIC PUBLISHERS**
Boston/Dordrecht/Lancaster

**Distributors for North, Central and South America:**
Kluwer Academic Publishers
101 Philip Drive
Assinippi Park
Norwell, Massachusetts 02061 USA
Telephone (781) 871-6600
Fax (781) 871-6528
E-Mail <kluwer@wkap.com>

**Distributors for all other countries:**
Kluwer Academic Publishers Group
Distribution Centre
Post Office Box 322
3300 AH Dordrecht, THE NETHERLANDS
Telephone 31 78 6392 392
Fax 31 78 6546 474
E-Mail <services@wkap.nl>

 Electronic Services <http://www.wkap.nl>

**Library of Congress Cataloging-in-Publication Data**
Tomita, Masaru.
  Efficient parsing for natural language.
  (The Kluwer international series in engineering and computer science;
SECS 8. Natural language processing and machine translation)
  Bibliography: p. Includes indexes.
  1. Parsing (Computer grammar) 2. Programming languages
(Electronic computers)--Semantics. 3. Algorithms. 4. Machine
translation. I. Title. II. Series: Kluwer international series in engineering
and computer science; SECS 8. III. Series: Kluwer international series
in engineering and computer science. Natural language processing and
machine translation.
P98.T65   1985   006.3'5   85-19834
ISBN 0-89838-202-5

*Printed on acid-free paper.*
Printed in the United States of America

*To Yuko*

昭和六十年五月

第二の故郷ピッツバーグにて

冨田　勝

# CONTENTS

# List of Figures

# List of Tables

# Preface

Parsing Efficiency is crucial when building *practical* natural language systems. This is especially the case for interactive systems such as natural language database access, interfaces to expert systems and interactive machine translation. Despite its importance, parsing efficiency has received little attention in the area of natural language processing. In the areas of compiler design and theoretical computer science, on the other hand, parsing algorithms have been evaluated primarily in terms of the theoretical worst case analysis (e.g. $O(n^3)$), and very few practical comparisons have been made.

This book introduces a context-free parsing algorithm that parses natural language more efficiently than any other existing parsing algorithms *in practice*. Its feasibility for use in practical systems is being proven in its application to Japanese language interface at Carnegie Group Inc., and to the continuous speech recognition project at Carnegie-Mellon University.

This work was done while I was pursuing a Ph.D degree at Carnegie-Mellon University. My advisers, Herb Simon and Jaime Carbonell, deserve many thanks for their unfailing support, advice and encouragement during my graduate studies. I would like to thank Phil Hayes and Ralph Grishman for their helpful comments and criticism that in many ways improved the quality of this book. I wish also to thank Steven Brooks for insightful comments on theoretical aspects of the book (chapter 4, appendices A, B and C), and Rich Thomason for improving the linguistic part of the book (the very beginning of section 1.1).

Special thanks go to the following professors in Japan for their suggestions that led to many useful ideas: Makoto Nagao, Toyoaki Nishida, Jun-ichi Tsujii, Hozumi Tanaka, Tetsunosuke Fujisaki, Hirosato Nomura, Shuji Doshita, Takehiro Tokuda, Osamu Watanabe and Masakazu Nakanishi. Professor Nagao gave me the opportunity to stay at Kyoto University in 1984. Many ideas presented in the book were developed during the stay.

Discussions with Bob Frederking and Hiroaki Saito also led to a number of useful ideas, and Noriyuki Nakatsuji helped me produce figures and graphs in this book. Cynthia Hibbard, a communication specialist, has given advice on my English writing for over three years. This book, as well as several previously published papers, was improved significantly by her suggestions.

I wish to express my appreciation to the Computer Science Department for accepting me as a graduate student, and for its full financial support during my years at CMU. I would like to acknowledge the following teachers who played key roles in my scholastic development during my grade school years: Shinya Nakagawa and Tadashi Nakayama.

Finally, I wish to thank Yuko Tomita for many discussions on linguistic aspects of my work, and more importantly, for her continuous encouragement and emotional support. Yuko always makes my life wonderful.

# EFFICIENT PARSING FOR NATURAL LANGUAGE

# Chapter 1
# Introduction

## 1.1. Motivation

This book introduces a context-free parsing algorithm which is especially efficient with natural language grammars. Context-free phrase structure has been used often in theoretical and practical systems for natural language processing. In transformational grammar, "deep structure", which is to be transformed into "surface structure", is generated by phrase structure rules called "base rules," that are usually required to be context-free [15, 28]. In Lexical Functional Grammar, underlying structures called "c-structures", from which "f-structures" are produced by functional operations, are again generated by context-free phrase structure rules [9]. In Unification Grammar, the base structure, on which unifications are performed, is generated by context-free phrase structure rules [32]. Perhaps most notably, in Generalized Phrase Structure Grammar, it is claimed that the syntax of natural language can be realized as a context-free grammar. Since the number of rules of such a grammar would be very large, the grammar is stated using "higher-level" operations, such as "meta-rules" and "rule-schemata" [23, 24]. Semantic grammar, which has been used successfully in practical systems including LIFER [35] and SOPHIE [10], is a context-free phrase structure grammar in which semantics as well as syntax is encoded in terminal and nonterminal symbols. Case frame parsing, which is used in PLUME [42], one of the first commercial natural language interfaces, appears to be least relevant to context-free phrase structure grammar. However, PLUME employs a large number of rules, called "rewriting rules," to specify low level structure which cannot be managed by case frames. These are very similar to context-free phrase structure rules.

In past decades, many context-free parsing algorithms have been developed, and they can be classified into two groups: algorithms for programming languages and algorithms for general context-free languages. The former group of algorithms are intended to handle only

1

a small subset of context-free grammars sufficient for programming languages. Such algorithms include the LL parsing algorithm, the operator precedence parsing algorithm, the predictive parsing algorithm and the LR parsing algorithm. They can handle only a subset of context-free grammars called LL grammars, operator precedence grammars, predictive grammars and LR grammars, respectively. These algorithms are tuned to handle a particular subset of context-free grammars, and therefore they are very efficient with their type of grammars. In other words, they take advantage of inherent features of the programming language.

The other group of algorithms, often called general context-free parsing algorithms, are designed to handle arbitrary context-free grammars. This group of algorithms includes Earley's algorithm and the Cocke-Younger-Kasami algorithm. General context-free languages include many difficult phenomena which never appear in programming languages, such as ambiguity and cycle. Algorithms in this group have not been widely used for programming languages, because their constant factors are too large to be used in practical compilers, as Earley admitted in his thesis [20]. This is not surprising, because those algorithms are not tuned for any particular subset of context-free grammars, and must be able to handle all the difficult phenomena in context-free grammars. In other words, they do not take advantage of inherent features of the programming language. Intuitively speaking, algorithms in this group are efficient for "hard" grammars by sacrificing efficiency on "easy" grammars.

No parsing algorithm has been designed that takes advantage of inherent features of natural languages. Because natural languages include somewhat more difficult phenomena than programming languages, we cannot simply use the first group of algorithms for natural languages. Natural languages are "harder" than programming languages, but they are still "easier" than general context-free languages. As we have seen above, we have context-free parsing algorithms at two extremes. The one is very efficient but not powerful enough to handle natural languages. The other is too powerful and turns out to be inefficient. We need something in between.

This book introduces such a context-free parsing algorithm, which can be viewed as an extended LR parsing algorithm. The fragile point of the standard LR parsing algorithm is that it cannot handle a non-LR grammar, even if the grammar is almost LR. Unlike the standard LR parsing algorithm, our algorithm can handle non-LR grammars with little loss of LR efficiency, if its grammar is "close" to LR. Fortunately, natural language grammars are considerably "closer" to LR than other general context-free grammars.

Experiments have shown that our algorithm is five to ten times faster than Earley's standard algorithm, with practical natural language grammars and sentences. Furthermore, like Earley's algorithm, our algorithm has two important characteristics:

- It parses a sentence strictly from left to right.
- It produces all possible parses out of an ambiguous sentence.

Neither of these characteristics has been appreciated in practical systems. However, later in this book, we suggest some practical applications of our algorithm, taking advantages of these two characteristics. Moreover, our algorithm is able to handle multi-part-of-speech words and unknown words without any special mechanism, as we will see in chapter 3.

## 1.2. Scope of the Book

Section 1.3 discusses the characteristics of natural language compared with programming language and general context-free language.

Chapter 2 gives the intuitive description of our algorithm. Section 2.2 reviews the standard LR parsing algorithm with an example. Section 2.3 extends the standard LR parsing algorithm with the idea of a graph-structured stack, so that it can handle natural language grammars. Section 2.4 describes how to represent parse trees efficiently, so that all possible parse trees (parse forest) take at most polynomial space as the ambiguity of a sentence grows exponentially.

In chapter 3, several examples are given. In section 3.1, the first example with a sentence "I saw a man in the park with a telescope" is presented to help the reader understand the algorithm more clearly. In section 3.2, the second example with a sentence "That information is important is doubtful" is presented to demonstrate that our algorithm is able to handle multi-part-of-speech words ("that", in the sentence) without any special means. In section 3.3, the third example is provided to show that our algorithm is also able to handle unknown words by considering an unknown word as a special multi-part-of-speech word whose part of speech can be anything.

In chapter 4, a more precise description of the algorithm is given. This chapter is, however, not intended to help the reader understand the algorithm. Chapter 4 may be skipped without loss of context. Section 4.2 defines the algorithm as a recognizer (i.e. no parse trees are produced), and section 4.3 then extends the recognition algorithm to produce parse trees.

In chapter 5, the relationship of our algorithm to the other algorithms for general context-free parsing is described. In section 5.1, the essential difference between our algorithm and others is identified. Section 5.2 then claims that our algorithm is more efficient than any others, as far as practical natural language processing is concerned. The section also presents a grammar with which our algorithm runs more slowly than the other general context-free algorithms. In section 5.3, the size of the parse forest representation is discussed. The only other algorithm that produces a polynomial sized parse forest without requiring a grammar to be Chomsky Normal Form is Earley's original algorithm in his thesis [20, 21]. Section 5.4, however, reveals the defect of Earley's original algorithm. We show that its parse forest representation is inadequate in some situations, and such defective situations can arise frequently in practice.

Chapter 6 presents several empirical results. In section 6.2, we implement our algorithm and test it against various grammars and sentences to verify its feasibility for use in practical systems. In section 6.3, we also implement Earley's algorithm and compare it with our algorithm, to support the claim that our algorithm is significantly more efficient than Earley's algorithm as far as practical natural language processing is concerned. Section 6.4 studies our algorithm's space efficiency in terms of the size of the parse forest, the size of graph-structured stack and the size of parsing tables. Section 6.5 concludes that in practical use our algorithm is feasible and more efficient than Earley's algorithm.

Chapters 7, 8 and 9 discuss several practical applications of the algorithm. Chapter 7 introduces the concept of on-line parsing, taking advantage of left-to-right-ness of our algorithm. The on-line parser starts parsing as soon as the user types in the first word of a sentence, without waiting the end of line. Several benefits of on-line parsing are described, and its application to user-friendly natural language interfaces is discussed.

Chapter 8 proposes a technique to disambiguate a sentence by asking the user interactively. After the user inputs a sentence and our parsing algorithm produces all possible parses, he is asked questions to choose his intended interpretation without being shown any parse trees. Section 8.2 describes a general technique of sentence disambiguation, called *explanation list comparison*. The technique can be applied to any context-free parsing algorithms. Although the technique presented in this section minimizes the questions to the user, it might be too general and too primitive. Application specific modifications may be required for it to be used in practical systems. Section 8.3 then describes a more specific and more efficient disambiguation algorithm that runs with our parsing algorithm and the shared-packed forest representation.

In chapter 9 an interactive/personal machine translation system is suggested. The machine translation system described in the chapter, which takes advantage of on-line parsing and interactive sentence disambiguation, has a totally different philosophy from that of conventional machine translation systems. We have implemented an experimental system by extending an existing English-Japanese machine translation system, to demonstrate feasibility of the interactive approach to machine translation. The pilot system is far away from being practical, but some promising data have been found from experiments with the system.

Finally, several concluding remarks are made in chapter 10, including a discussion of possible future work in this area.

## 1.3. Characteristics of Natural Language

It is important to describe some characteristics of natural language briefly at the beginning of the book. In this section, we compare natural languages with programming languages and general context-free languages. Since it is impossible to mention all characteristics, only those which are relevant to the book are described.

First of all, natural languages are inherently ambiguous, whereas programming language are not ambiguous. A language is *ambiguous*, if it includes ambiguous sentences. A sentence is *ambiguous*, if it has two or more parses. In programming languages, a sentence must always have at most one parse. In natural languages, on the other hand, one sentence can have multiple parses. At the syntax level, the number of parses of an ambiguous sentence sometimes exceeds a thousand. Ideally, the parser should produce only one parse out of a syntactically ambiguous sentence, using semantics, pragmatics and/or heuristics. However, not all ambiguity problems can be solved by those techniques at the current state of art. Moreover, some sentences are absolutely ambiguous, that is, even a human cannot disambiguate them. In the case where there exist two or more possible parses, it is not acceptable for a practical natural language parser to produce only one arbitrary parse. All possible parses should be produced and stored somewhere for later disambiguation. The existence of ambiguity is the biggest difference between programming languages and natural languages. Because no programming language parsing algorithm can handle ambiguity, none can be used for natural language parsing.

Some parsing algorithms for programming languages require their grammar to be non-left-recursive and/or non-empty. A *left-recursive grammar* is a grammar with a rule; A -> A B. An *empty grammar* is a grammar with a rule; A -> e. In natural language grammars, both phenomena are likely to appear, as one often writes rules like:

NP -> NP PP
VP -> VP PP

to represent prepositional phrase attachment, and

NP -> e

to represent NP deletion. Thus, natural language parsing algorithms should be capable of handling these two phenomena.

Next, we compare general context-free language with natural language. General context-free language grammars include several phenomena which seldom or never appear in natural language grammars. For example, it is extremely unlikely for a natural language grammar to include "densely" ambiguous grammar rules as the following.

```
S --> S S S S
S --> S S S
S --> S S
S --> x
```

sentence = 'xxxxxx'

**Figure 1-1:**  Dense Ambiguity

Also, the following two phenomena never appear in natural language grammars.

```
S --> S S
S --> e          (e = null string)
S --> x
```

sentence = 'xxx'

**Figure 1-2:**  Infinite Ambiguity

```
S --> S
S --> x
```

sentence = 'x'

**Figure 1-3:**  Cyclic Grammar

A grammar is *infinitely* ambiguous, if it produces an infinite number of parses with some input sentences. A grammar is *cyclic*, if there exists a nonterminal which can be reduced to itself.[1] General context-free parsing algorithms must be capable of handling these "hard" grammars efficiently. In natural language parsing, however, we can simply disregard these problems.

There are two more characteristics of natural language worth mentioning here. First, the length of a sentence (the number of words) is usually between 10 and 20, and seldom exceeds 30. Second, the number of rules in a natural language grammar gets large if one tries to cover the language fairly comprehensively. No accurate estimation has been made on how many context-free rules are needed to cover English almost completely. We know, however, that it is much larger than for programming language grammars. Therefore, a natural language parser must be efficient with respect not only to the sentence length, but also to the number of rules in its grammar.

The next chapter starts to describe our parsing algorithm for natural languages. The discussion in this section becomes highly relevant when we evaluate the algorithm's performance in later chapters.

## 1.4. Previous Work

A primitive version of the algorithm was described in the author's previous work [49]. Because the primitive algorithm used a "tree-structured stack", exponential time was required in the worst case to find all parses. However, the current algorithm uses the "graph-structured stack" and runs in polynomial time. Also, the primitive algorithm was a recognizer; that is, it did not produce any parses, while the current algorithm produces all possible parses in an efficient representation. A "graph-structured stack" was proposed in the author's more recent work [52]. The algorithm was previously called the *MLR* parsing algorithm. All ideas presented in those two previous papers are included in this book, and the reader does not need to refer to them to understand the current discussion.

---

[1] These two phenomena are equivalent; a grammar is infinitely ambiguous if and only if a grammar is cyclic.

# Chapter 2
# Informal Description of the Algorithm

## 2.1. Introduction

This chapter gives an informal description of our algorithm. First, we review the standard LR parsing algorithm with an example. Then, section 2.3 extends the standard LR parsing algorithm with the idea of a graph-structured stack, so that it can handle natural language grammars. Finally, section 2.4 describes how to represent all possible parse trees efficiently, so that as the ambiguity of a sentence grows exponentially, it takes at most polynomial space to represent them.

## 2.2. The LR parsing Algorithm

As mentioned in section 1.3, The LR parsing algorithms [1, 2] were developed originally for programming languages. An LR parsing algorithm is a shift-reduce parsing algorithm which is deterministically guided by a parsing table indicating what action should be taken next. The parsing table can be obtained automatically from a context-free phrase structure grammar, using an algorithm first developed by DeRemer [18, 19]. We do not describe the algorithm here, referring the reader to chapter 6 in Aho and Ullman [4]. Appendix A in this book also contains a brief description of the LR parsing table construction algorithm.

### 2.2.1. An example

An example grammar and its LR parsing table obtained by the algorithm are shown in Figure 2-1 and 2-2, respectively.

Grammar symbols starting with "*" represent pre-terminals. Entries "sh *n*" in the action table (the left part of the table) indicate the action "shift one word from input buffer onto the

```
-----------------------------------
(1)    S  --> NP VP
(2)    S  --> S PP
(3)    NP --> *det *n
(4)    PP --> *prep NP
(5)    VP --> *v NP
-----------------------------------
```

Figure 2-1: Example Grammar

| State | *det | *n | *v | *prep | $ | | NP | PP | VP | S |
|---|---|---|---|---|---|---|---|---|---|---|
| 0 | sh3 | | | | | | 2 | | | 1 |
| 1 | | | | sh5 | acc | | | 4 | | |
| 2 | | | sh6 | | | | | | 7 | |
| 3 | | sh8 | | | | | | | | |
| 4 | | | | re2 | re2 | | | | | |
| 5 | sh3 | | | | | | 9 | | | |
| 6 | sh3 | | | | | | 10 | | | |
| 7 | | | | re1 | re1 | | | | | |
| 8 | | re3 | | re3 | re3 | | | | | |
| 9 | | | | re4 | re4 | | | | | |
| 10 | | | | re5 | re5 | | | | | |

action table                    goto table

Figure 2-2: LR Parsing Table

stack, and go to state *n*". Entries "re *n*" indicate the action "reduce constituents on the stack using rule *n*". The entry "acc" stands for the action "accept", and blank spaces represent "error". The goto table (the right part of the table) decides to what state the parser should go after a reduce action. The exact definition and operation of the LR parser can be found in Aho and Ullman [4].

Let us parse a simple sentence "My car has a radio" using the LR parsing table. The trace of the LR parsing algorithm is shown in Figure 2-3.[2]

The number on the top (rightmost) of the stack indicates the current state. Initially, the current state is 0. The inputbuffer initially contains the input sentence followed by the end marker "$".

Since the parser is looking at the word "MY", whose category is "*det", the next action "shift and goto state 3" is determined from the action table. The parser takes the word "MY" away from the inputbuffer, pushes the preterminal "*det" onto the stack, and goes to state 3 pushing the number "3" onto the stack. The inputbuffer is now "CAR HAS A RADIO $".

---

[2]No parse tree is produced.

Inputbuffer = MY CAR HAS A RADIO $

| STACK | NA | NW |
|-------|-----|-------|
| 0 | sh3 | MY |
| 0 *det 3 | sh8 | CAR |
| 0 *det 3 *n 8 | re3 | HAS |
| 0 NP 2 | sh6 | HAS |
| 0 NP 2 *v 6 | sh3 | A |
| 0 NP 2 *v 6 *det 3 | sh8 | RADIO |
| 0 NP 2 *v 6 *det 3 *n 8 | re3 | $ |
| 0 NP 2 *v 6 NP 10 | re5 | $ |
| 0 NP 2 VP 7 | re1 | $ |
| 0 S 1 | acc | $ |

**Figure 2-3:** Trace of LR Parsing

The next word the parser is looking at is "CAR", whose category is "*n", and "shift and goto state 8" is determined from the action table as the next action. Thus, the parser takes the word "CAR" from the inputbuffer, pushes the preterminal "*n", and goes to state 8 pushing the number "8" onto the stack. The inputbuffer is now "HAS A RADIO $".

The next word is "HAS", and from the action table, "reduce using rule 3" is determined as the next action. So, the parser reduces the stack using the rule "NP --> *det *n". After popping the constituents, *det and *n, out of the stack, "0" is on the top of the stack. Because we are pushing "NP" on to the stack, state 2 is determined as the current state by looking at row 0 and column "NP" of the goto table. The inputbuffer is still "HAS A RADIO $", because we have not shifted the word "HAS" yet.

Since the parser is still looking at the word "HAS", and it is in state 2, the next action is "shift and goto state 6". So, the parser shifts the word "HAS" from the inputbuffer onto the stack, and goes to state 6.

Several steps later, the parser eventually finds the action "accept", which is the signal for the parser to halt the process.

### 2.2.2. Problem in Applying to Natural Languages

As we have seen in the example, the LR paring is one of the most efficient parsing algorithms. It is totally deterministic and no backtracking or search is involved. The algorithm to build an LR parsing table is well-established, and implemented in a practical program called YACC (Yet Another Compiler Compiler) [29] running on Unix.

Unfortunately, we cannot directly adopt the LR parsing technique for natural languages. This is because not all context-free phrase structure grammars (CFPSG's) can have an LR parsing table. Only a small subset of CFPSG's called *LR grammars* (see figure 2-4) can have such an LR parsing table. Every ambiguous grammar is not LR, for example. Since natural language grammars are almost always ambiguous, we cannot have an LR parsing table for natural language grammars.

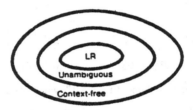

Figure 2-4: Context-free Grammars and LR grammars

If a grammar is non-LR, its parsing table will have multiple entries[3] ; one or more of the action table entries will be multiply defined. Figures 2-5 and 2-6 show an example of a non-LR grammar and its parsing table.

```
----------------------------------
  (1)    S  --> NP VP
  (2)    S  --> S PP
  (3)   NP  --> *n
  (4)   NP  --> *det *n
  (5)   NP  --> NP PP
  (6)   PP  --> *prep NP
  (7)   VP  --> *v NP
----------------------------------
```

Figure 2-5: An Example Ambiguous Grammar

---

[3] They are often called *conflicts*.

| State | *det | *n | *v | *prep | $ | NP | PP | VP | S |
|---|---|---|---|---|---|---|---|---|---|
| 0 | sh3 | sh4 | | | | 2 | | | 1 |
| 1 | | | | sh6 | acc | | 5 | | |
| 2 | | | sh7 | sh6 | | | 9 | 8 | |
| 3 | | sh10 | | | | | | | |
| 4 | | | re3 | re3 | re3 | | | | |
| 5 | | | | re2 | re2 | | | | |
| 6 | sh3 | sh4 | | | | 11 | | | |
| 7 | sh3 | sh4 | | | | 12 | | | |
| 8 | | | | re1 | re1 | | | | |
| 9 | | | re5 | re5 | re5 | | | | |
| 10 | | | re4 | re4 | re4 | | | | |
| 11 | | | re6 | re6,sh6 | re6 | | 9 | | |
| 12 | | | | re7,sh6 | re7 | | 9 | | |

Figure 2-6: LR Parsing Table with Multiple Entries

We can see that there are two multiple entries in the action table; on the rows of state 11 and 12 at the column labeled "*prep". It has been thought that, for LR parsing, multiple entries are fatal because once a parsing table has multiple entries, deterministic parsing is no longer possible and some kind of non-determinism is necessary. However, in this book, we shall introduce an extended LR parsing algorithm that can handle parsing tables with multiple entries using a "graph-structured" stack. Our parsing algorithm, while it can apply to non-LR grammars, preserves most of the efficiency of the standard LR parsing algorithm.

## 2.3. Handling Multiple Entries

As mentioned above, once a parsing table has multiple entries, deterministic parsing is no longer possible and some kind of non-determinism is necessary. We handle multiple entries with a special technique, named a *graph-structured stack*. In order to introduce the concept, we first give a simpler form of non-determinism, and make refinements on it. Subsection 2.3.1 describes a simple and straightforward non-deterministic technique, i.e. pseudo-parallelism (breath-first search), in which the system maintains a number of stacks simultaneously, called the *Stack List*. A disadvantage of the stack list is then described. The next subsection describes the idea of stack combination, which was introduced in the author's earlier research [49], to make the algorithm much more efficient. With this idea, stacks are represented as trees (or a forest). Finally, a further refinement, the graph-structured stack, is described to make the algorithm even more efficient; efficient enough to run in polynomial time.

## 2.3.1. With Stack List

The simplest idea is to handle multiple entries non-deterministically. We adopt pseudo-parallelism (breath-first search), maintaining a list of stacks called a *Stack List*. The pseudo-parallelism works as follows.

A number of *processes* are operated in parallel. Each process has a stack and behaves basically the same as in standard LR parsing. When a process encounters a multiple entry, the process is split into several processes (one for each entry), by replicating its stack. When a process encounters an error entry, the process is killed, by removing its stack from the stack list. All processes are synchronized; they shift a word at the same time so that they always look at the same word. Thus, if a process encounters a shift action, it waits until all other processes also encounter a (possibly different) shift action.

Figure 2-7 shows a snapshot of the stack list right after shifting the word "with" in the sentence "I saw a man on the bed in the apartment with a telescope" using the grammar in figure 2-5 and the parsing table in figure 2-6. For the sake of convenience, we denote a stack with vertices and edges. The leftmost vertex is the bottom of the stack, and the rightmost vertex is the top of the stack. Vertices represented by a circle are called *state vertices*, and they represent a state number. Vertices represented by a square are called *symbol vertices*, and they represent a grammar symbol. Each stack is exactly the same as a stack in the standard LR parsing algorithm. The distance between vertices (length of an edge) does not have any significance, except it may help the reader understand the status of the stacks.

We notice that some stacks in the stack list appear to be identical. They are, however, internally different because they have reached the current state in different ways. Although we shall describe a method to compress them into one stack in the next section, we consider them to be different in this section.

A disadvantage of the stack list method is that there are no interconnections between stacks (processes) and there is no way in which a process can utilize what other processes have done already. The number of stacks in the stack list grows exponentially as ambiguities are encountered.[4] For example, these 14 processes in figure 2-7 will parse the rest of the sentence "the telescope" 14 times in exactly the same way. This can be avoided by using a tree-structured stack, which is described in the following subsection.

---

[4]Although it is possibly reduced if some processes reach error entries and die.

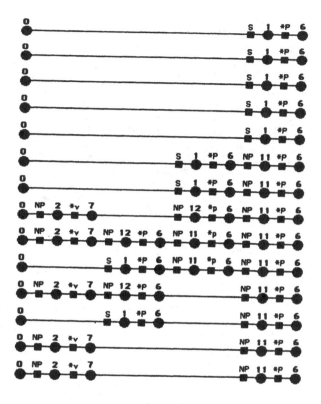

Figure 2-7:  Stack List

## 2.3.2. With a Tree-structured Stack

If two processes are in a common state, that is, if two stacks have a common state number at the rightmost vertex, they will behave in exactly the same manner until the vertex is popped from the stacks by a reduce action.  To avoid this redundant operation, these processes are unified into one process by combining their stacks.  Whenever two or more processes have a common state number on the top of their stacks, the top vertices are unified, and these stacks are represented as a tree, where the top vertex corresponds to the root of the tree.  We call this a tree-structured stack.  When the top vertex is popped, the tree-structured stack is split into the original number of stacks.  In general, the system maintains a number of tree-structured stacks in parallel, so stacks are represented as a forest.  Figure 2-8 shows a

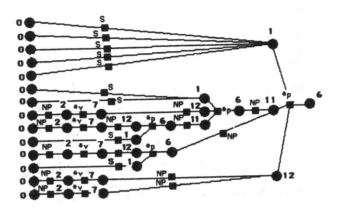

**Figure 2-8:** A Tree-structured Stack

snapshot of the tree-structured stack immediately after shifting the word "with". Although the amount of computation is significantly reduced by the stack combination technique, the number of branches of the tree-structured stack (the number of bottoms of the stack) that must be maintained still grows exponentially as ambiguities are encountered. In the next subsection, we describe a further modification in which stacks are represented as a directed acyclic graph, in order to avoid such inefficiency.

### 2.3.3. With a Graph-structured Stack

So far, when a stack is split, a copy of the whole stack is made. However, we do not necessarily have to copy the whole stack: Even after different parallel operations on the tree-structured stack, the bottom portion of the stack may remain the same. Only the necessary portion of the stack should therefore be split. When a stack is split, the stack is thus represented as a tree, where the bottom of the stack corresponds to the root of the tree. With the stack combination technique described in the previous subsection, stacks are represented as a directed acyclic graph. Figure 2-9 shows a snapshot of the graph-structured stack. It is easy to show that the algorithm with the graph-structured stack does not parse any part of an input sentence more than once in the same way. This is because if two processes had parsed a part of a sentence in the same way, they would have been in the same state, and

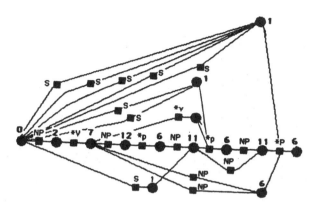

**Figure 2-9:** A Graph-Structured Stack

they would have been combined as one process.[5]  So far, we have focussed on how to accept or reject a sentence. In practice, however, the parser must not only simply accept or reject sentences, but also build the syntactic structure(s) of the sentence (parse forest). The next section describes how to represent the parse forest and how to build it with our parsing algorithm.

## 2.4. An Efficient Representation of a Parse Forest

As briefly discussed in section 1.3, it is desirable for practical natural language parsers to produce all possible parses and store them somewhere for later disambiguation, in case an input sentence is ambiguous. The ambiguity (the number of parses) of a sentence grows exponentially as the length of a sentence grows [16]. Thus, one might notice that, even with an efficient parsing algorithm such as the one we described, the parser would take exponential time because exponential time would be required merely to print out all parse trees (parse forest). We must therefore provide an efficient representation so that the size of the parse forest does not grow exponentially.

This section describes two techniques for providing an efficient representation: sub-tree

---

[5] The graph-structured stack looks very similar to a chart in chart parsing. In fact, we can view our algorithm as an extended chart parsing algorithm which is guided by LR parsing tables. The major extension is that nodes in the chart contain more information (LR state numbers) than in conventional chart parsing. We do not discuss this matter further.

sharing and local ambiguity packing. It should be mentioned that these two techniques are not completely new ideas, and some existing systems already adopted these techniques. To the author's knowledge, however, no existing system has adopted both techniques at the same time.

### 2.4.1. Sub-tree Sharing

If two or more trees have a common sub-tree, the sub-tree should be represented only once. For example, the parse forest for the sentence "I saw a man with a telescope" should be represented as follows:

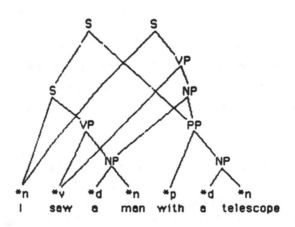

**Figure 2-10:** Shared Forest

Our parsing algorithm is very well suited for building this kind of shared forest as its output, as we shall see in the following.

To implement this, we no longer push grammatical symbols on the stack; instead, we push pointers to a node of the shared forest. (The term *node* is used for forest representation, whereas the term *vertex* is used for graph-structured stack representation.) When the parser "shifts" a word, it creates a leaf node labeled with the word and the pre-terminal, and instead of pushing the pre-terminal symbol, a pointer to the newly created leaf node is pushed onto the stack. If the exact same leaf node (i.e. the node labeled with the same word and the same pre-terminal) already exists, a pointer to this existing node is pushed onto the stack, without creating another node. When the parser "reduces" the stack, it pops pointers from the stack, creates a new node whose successive nodes are pointed to by those popped pointers, and pushes a pointer to the newly created node onto the stack.

Using this relatively simple procedure, our parsing algorithm can produce the shared forest as its output without any other special book-keeping mechanism, because it never does the same reduce action twice in the same manner.

### 2.4.2. Local Ambiguity Packing

We say that two or more subtrees represent *local ambiguity* if they have common leaf nodes and their top nodes are labeled with the same non-terminal symbol. That is to say, a fragment of a sentence is locally ambiguous if the fragment can be reduced to a certain non-terminal symbol in two or more ways. If a sentence has many local ambiguities, the total ambiguity would grow exponentially. To avoid this, we use a technique called *local ambiguity packing*, which works in the following way. The top nodes of subtrees that represent local ambiguity are merged and treated by higher-level structures as if there were only one node. Such a node is called a *packed node*, and nodes before packing are called *subnodes* of the packed node. Examples of a shared forest without and with local ambiguity packing are shown in figure 2-11 and 2-12, respectively. Packed nodes are represented by boxes. We have three packed nodes in figure 2-12; one with three subnodes and two with two subnodes.

Local ambiguity packing can be easily implemented with our parsing algorithm as follows. In the graph-structured stack, if two or more symbol vertices have a common state vertex immediately on their left and a common state vertex immediately on their right, they represent local ambiguity. Nodes pointed to by these symbol vertices are to be packed as one node. In figure 2-9 for example, we see one 5-way local ambiguity and two 2-way local ambiguities.

The algorithm will be made clear by examples in the next chapter.

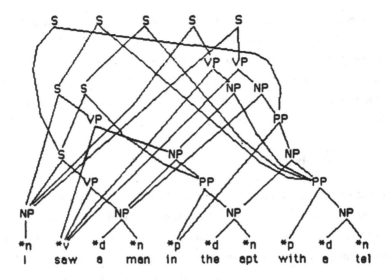

Figure 2-11: Unpacked Shared Forest

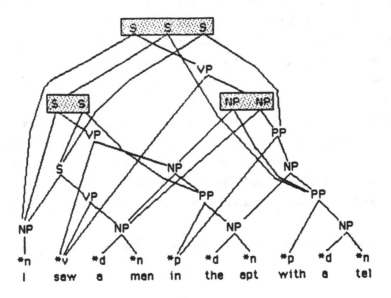

Figure 2-12: Packed Shared Forest

# Chapter 3
# Examples

---

## 3.1. Introduction

This chapter presents three examples. The first example, using the sentence "I saw a man in the apartment with a telescope", is intended to help the reader understand the algorithm more clearly. (Throughout this book, the shorter words, "park" and "scope", will be occasionally used in stead of "apartment" and "telescope", respectively, for purposes of convenience.) A reader who has not clearly understood the algorithm from chapter 2 should understand it here. Although we give a formal specification of the algorithm in chapter 4, it is provided mainly for proving correctness of the algorithm in appendix B, and is not intended to help the reader understand the algorithm.

The second example, with the sentence "That information is important is doubtful", is presented to demonstrate that our algorithm is able to handle multi-part-of-speech words without any special mechanism. In the sentence, "that" is a multi-part-of-speech word, because it could also be a determiner or a pronoun.

The third example is provided to show that the algorithm is also able to handle unknown words by considering an unknown word as a special multi-part-of-speech word whose part of speech can be anything. We use an example sentence "I * a *", where *'s represent unknown words.

## 3.2. The Example

This section gives a trace of the algorithm with the grammar in figure 2-5, the parsing table in figure 2-6 and the sentence "I saw a man in the park with a scope." The grammar and the parsing table are presented here as well.

```
-----------------------------------
(1)   S  --> NP VP
(2)   S  --> S PP
(3)   NP --> *n
(4)   NP --> *det *n
(5)   NP --> NP PP
(6)   PP --> *prep NP
(7)   VP --> *v NP
-----------------------------------
```

Figure 2-5: An Example Ambiguous Grammar

| State | *det | *n | *v | *prep | $ | | NP | PP | VP | S |
|-------|------|-----|------|---------|---------|---|-----|----|----|---|
| 0 | sh3 | sh4 | | | | | 2 | | | 1 |
| 1 | | | | sh6 | acc | | 5 | | | |
| 2 | | | sh7 | sh6 | | | | 9 | 8 | |
| 3 | | sh10 | | | | | | | | |
| 4 | | | re3 | re3 | re3 | | | | | |
| 5 | | | | re2 | re2 | | | | | |
| 6 | sh3 | sh4 | | | | | 11 | | | |
| 7 | sh3 | sh4 | | | | | 12 | | | |
| 8 | | | | re1 | re1 | | | | | |
| 9 | | | re5 | re5 | re5 | | | | | |
| 10 | | | re4 | re4 | re4 | | | | | |
| 11 | | | re6 | re6,sh6 | re6 | | | 9 | | |
| 12 | | | | re7,sh6 | re7 | | | 9 | | |

Figure 2-6: LR Parsing Table with Multiple Entries

In each step in the trace, the following four things are shown.

- The graph-structured stack. Each node in the graph-structured stack is called a *vertex*, to distinguish it from *nodes* in the parse forest. There are two kinds of vertices. Vertices represented by a circle are called *state vertices*, and they indicate state numbers. Vertices represented by a square are called *symbol vertices*, and they are pointers to a particular node in the parse forest. The right-most vertices are called *top vertices*.

- The parse forest. It is represented as an array, where each element represents a node in the parse forest. An element of the array is either a list of a preterminal symbol and a word, in the case where the element represents a leaf node, or else a list of a nonterminal symbol and one or more subnodes. A subnode consists of a list of its successive nodes.

- The next actions. The next actions are represented in angle blankets, and they are associated with a top vertex in the stack. Note that there may be more than one next action on one top vertex, due to multiple entries. Also, there may be more than one top vertex at one time.

- The next word to be parsed in the input sentence.

At the very beginning, the stack contains only one vertex labeled 0, and the parse forest contains nothing. By looking at the action table, the next action "shift 4" is determined as in standard LR parsing.

Next Word = 'I'        **0**
                        ● **[sh 4]**

Figure 3-1:  Trace of the Parser

When shifting the word "I", the algorithm creates a leaf node in the parse forest labeled with the word "I" and its preterminal "*n", and pushes a pointer to the leaf node onto the stack. The next action "reduce 3" (reduce using the rule NP -> *n) is determined from the action table.

Next Word = 'saw'     **0  0  4**
                       ●─■─● **[re 3]**                    0 [*n 'I']

Figure 3-2:  Trace of the Parser (cont.)

We reduce the stack basically in the same manner as standard LR parsing. It pops the top vertex "4" and the pointer "0" from the stack, and creates a new node in the parse forest whose successor is the node pointed to by the pointer. The newly created node is labeled with the left hand side symbol of rule 3, namely "NP". The pointer to this newly created node, namely "1", is pushed onto the stack. The action "shift 7" is determined as the next action. Now, we have figure 3-3.

Next Word = 'saw'     **0  1  2**
                       ●─■─● **[sh 7]**                    0 [*n 'I']
                                                           1 [NP (0)]

Figure 3-3:  Trace of the Parser (cont.)

After executing "shift 7", we have figure 3-4.

Next Word = 'a'

```
   0  1  2  2  7
   ●──■──●──■──● [sh 3]
```

```
0 [*n 'I']
1 [NP (0)]
2 [*v 'saw']
```

**Figure 3-4:** Trace of the Parser (cont.)

After executing "shift 3", we have figure 3-5.

Next Word = 'man'

```
   0  1  2  2  7  3  3
   ●──■──●──■──●──■──● [sh 10]
```

```
0 [*n 'I']
1 [NP (0)]
2 [*v 'saw']
3 [*det 'a']
```

**Figure 3-5:** Trace of the Parser (cont.)

After executing "shift 10", we have figure 3-6.

Next Word = 'in'

```
   0  1  2  2  7  3  3  4  10
   ●──■──●──■──●──■──●──■──● [re 4]
```

```
0 [*n 'I']
1 [NP (0)]
2 [*v 'saw']
3 [*det 'a']
4 [*n 'man']
```

**Figure 3-6:** Trace of the Parser (cont.)

The next action is "reduce 4" (reduce using the rule NP -> *det *n). It pops pointers, "3" and "4", and creates a new node in the parse forest such that node 3 and node 4 are its successors. The newly created node is labeled with the left hand side symbol of rule 4, i.e. "NP". The pointer to this newly created node, "5", is pushed onto the stack, and state 12 is determined as the current state by the goto table. We now have figure 3-7.

At this point, we encounter a multiple entry, "reduce 7" and "shift 6", and both actions are to be executed. Reduce actions are always executed first, and shift actions are executed only when there is no reduce action to execute. After executing "reduce 7", the stack and the parse forest are as in figure 3-8. The top vertex labeled "12" is not popped away, because it

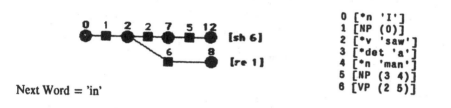

**Figure 3-7:** Trace of the Parser (cont.)

still has an action which is not yet executed. Such a top vertex, or more generally, vertices with one or more actions yet to be executed, are called *active*. Thus, we have two active vertices in the stack in figure 3-8: one labeled "12", and the other labeled "8". The action "reduce 1" is determined from the action table, and is associated with the latter vertex.

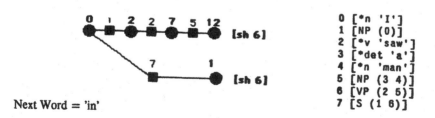

**Figure 3-8:** Trace of the Parser (cont.)

Because, as mentioned, reduce actions have a higher priority than shift actions, the algorithm next executes "reduce 1" on the vertex labeled "8". The action "shift 6" is determined from the action table (figure 3-9).

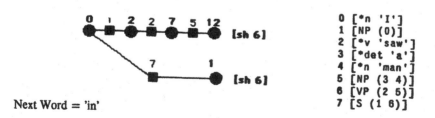

**Figure 3-9:** Trace of the Parser (cont.)

Now we have two "shift 6"'s. Because both actions are to shift the same word "in" as the same grammatical category "*prep", the parser creates only one new leaf node in the parse forest. After executing two shift actions, it combines vertices in the stack wherever possible. The stack and the parse forest are as in figure 3-10, and "shift 3" is determined from the action table as the next action.

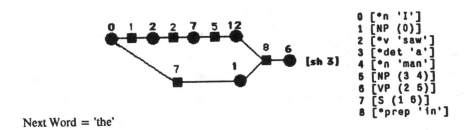

Next Word = 'the'

**Figure 3-10:** Trace of the Parser (cont.)

After executing "shift 3", we have figure 3-11.

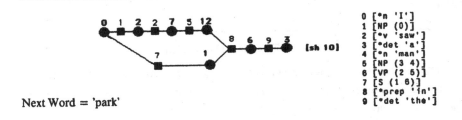

Next Word = 'park'

**Figure 3-11:** Trace of the Parser (cont.)

After executing "shift 10", we have figure 3-12.

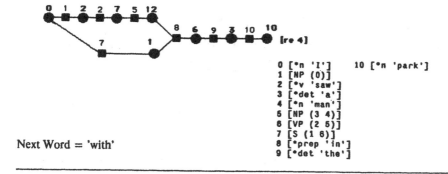

**Figure 3-12:** Trace of the Parser (cont.)

After executing "reduce 4", we have figure 3-13.

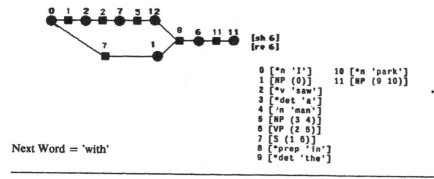

**Figure 3-13:** Trace of the Parser (cont.)

At this point, we encounter a multiple entry again. It executes "reduce 6" first. Note that, although executing "reduce 6" creates two new active vertices, only one node (12) needs to be created in the parse forest.

Now we have three active vertices, as shown in figure 3-14. Because there are two reduce actions, "reduce 5" on the second active vertex is arbitrarily chosen as the action to execute next.

After executing "reduce 5", we have figure 3-15. It encounters a multiple entry again, and "reduce 7" is arbitrarily chosen over "reduce 2" as the next action to execute.

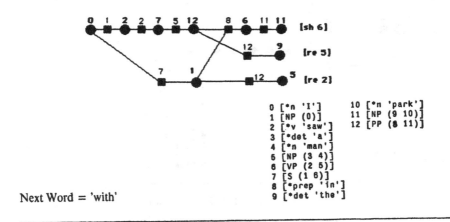

Next Word = 'with'

**Figure 3-14:** Trace of the Parser (cont.)

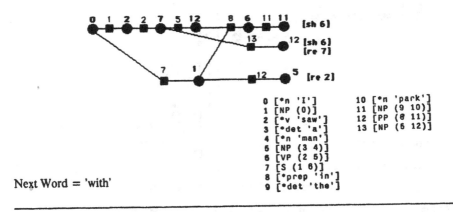

Next Word = 'with'

**Figure 3-15:** Trace of the Parser (cont.)

Now we have four active vertices as shown in figure 3-16, and "reduce 1" is arbitrarily chosen over "reduce 2" as the next action to execute. After executing "reduce 1", we have figure 3-17.

Then, "reduce 2" is executed because it is the only reduce action. After executing the reduce action, the algorithm would create a new active vertex labeled "1". However, since there already exists a top vertex labeled "1", the new vertex and the existing vertex would be combined as in figure 3-18.

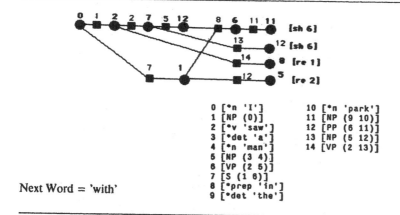

Next Word = 'with'

**Figure 3-16:** Trace of the Parser (cont.)

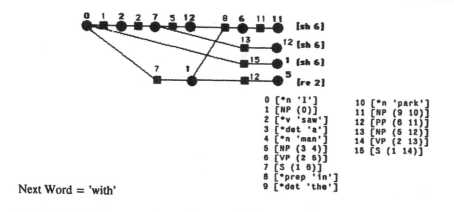

Next Word = 'with'

**Figure 3-17:** Trace of the Parser (cont.)

Furthermore, since both come immediately from the same state vertex (i.e. the vertex labeled "0"), they represent a local ambiguity. They are therefore packed as in figure 3-19.

Now, the algorithm executes three shift actions, creating only one leaf node in the parse forest. After executing the shift actions, vertices in the stack are combined wherever possible, and we have figure 3-20.

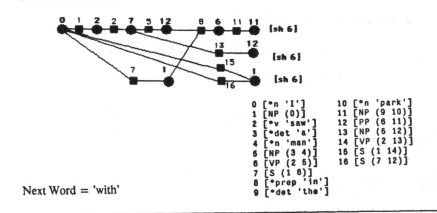

```
0 [•n 'I']          10 [•n 'park']
1 [NP (0)]          11 [NP (9 10)]
2 [•v 'saw']        12 [PP (6 11)]
3 [•det 'a']        13 [NP (5 12)]
4 [•n 'man']        14 [VP (2 13)]
5 [NP (3 4)]        15 [S (1 14)]
6 [VP (2 5)]        16 [S (7 12)]
7 [S (1 6)]
8 [•prep 'in']
9 [•det 'the']
```

Next Word = 'with'

**Figure 3-18:** Trace of the Parser (cont.)

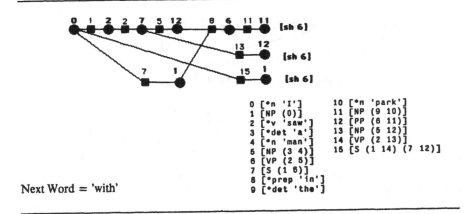

```
0 [•n 'I']          10 [•n 'park']
1 [NP (0)]          11 [NP (9 10)]
2 [•v 'saw']        12 [PP (6 11)]
3 [•det 'a']        13 [NP (5 12)]
4 [•n 'man']        14 [VP (2 13)]
5 [NP (3 4)]        15 [S (1 14) (7 12)]
6 [VP (2 5)]
7 [S (1 6)]
8 [•prep 'in']
9 [•det 'the']
```

Next Word = 'with'

**Figure 3-19:** Trace of the Parser (cont.)

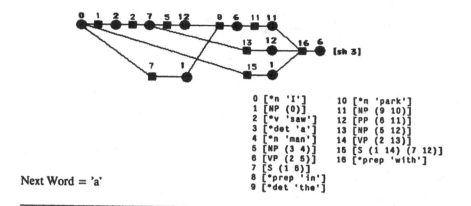

**Figure 3-20:** Trace of the Parser (cont.)

After executing "shift 3", we have figure 3-21.

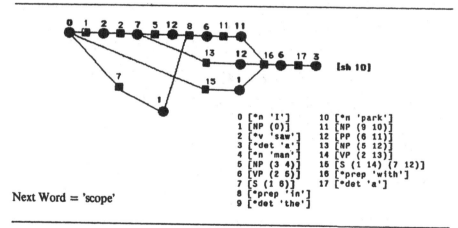

**Figure 3-21:** Trace of the Parser (cont.)

After executing "shift 10", we have figure 3-22.

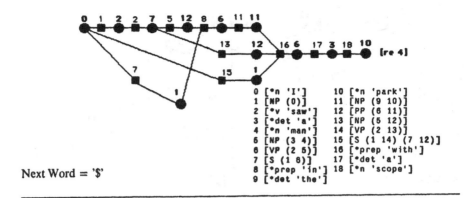

Figure 3-22: Trace of the Parser (cont.)

After executing "reduce 4", we have figure 3-23.

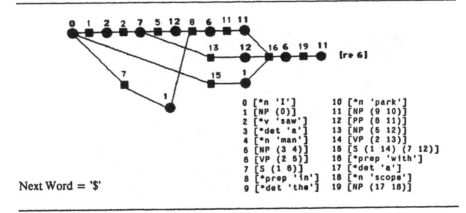

Figure 3-23: Trace of the Parser (cont.)

After executing "reduce 6", the algorithm would create three new top vertices, but combining vertices wherever possible, we have figure 3-24.

Now, there are two active vertices, and the action "reduce 5" is arbitrarily chosen as the next action to execute. Looking back from the top vertex labeled "9", we can think of two ways to execute the reduce action. After executing one of the ways, we have figure 3-25, and after executing the other, we have figure 3-26.

Now there are three active vertices, and "reduce 6" on the first top vertex is arbitrarily

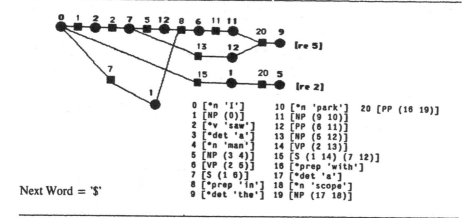

**Figure 3-24:** Trace of the Parser (cont.)

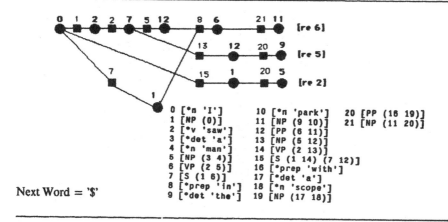

**Figure 3-25:** Trace of the Parser (cont.)

chosen as the next action to execute. After executing the reduce action, the algorithm would create two new top vertices, but one is combined with the one which already exists (figure 3-27).

The action "reduce 5" on the first top vertex is arbitrarily chosen as the next action to execute. It would create a new top vertex labeled "12", but the vertex is combined with the one which already exists. Furthermore, since both vertices come immediately from the same state vertex (i.e. the one labeled "7"), they represent a local ambiguity. Thus, instead of

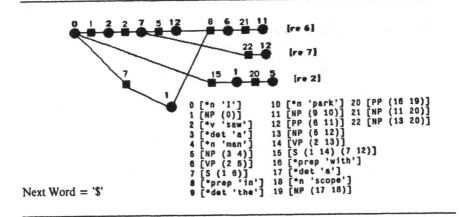

Next Word = '$'

**Figure 3-26:** Trace of the Parser (cont.)

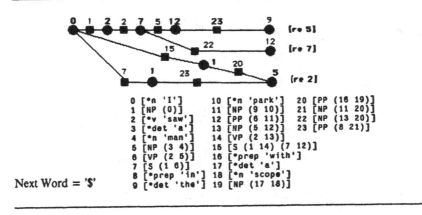

Next Word = '$'

**Figure 3-27:** Trace of the Parser (cont.)

creating a new node in the parse forest, we add a subnode "(5 23)" to node 22, which already exists in the parse forest (figure 3-28).

After executing "reduce 7" on the top vertex labeled "12", we have figure 3-29.

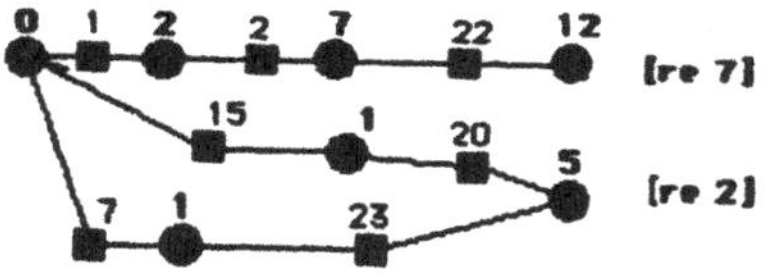

```
0  [*n 'I']        10 [*n 'park']     20 [PP (16 19)]
1  [NP (0)]        11 [NP (9 10)]     21 [NP (11 20)]
2  [*v 'saw']      12 [PP (6 11)]     22 [NP (13 20) (5 23)]
3  [*det 'a']      13 [NP (5 12)]     23 [PP (8 21)]
4  [*n 'man']      14 [VP (2 13)]
5  [NP (3 4)]      15 [S (1 14) (7 12)]
6  [VP (2 5)]      16 [*prep 'with']
7  [S (1 6)]       17 [*det 'a']
8  [*prep 'in']    18 [*n 'scope']
9  [*det 'the']    19 [NP (17 18)]
```

Next Word = '$'

Figure 3-28:  Trace of the Parser (cont.)

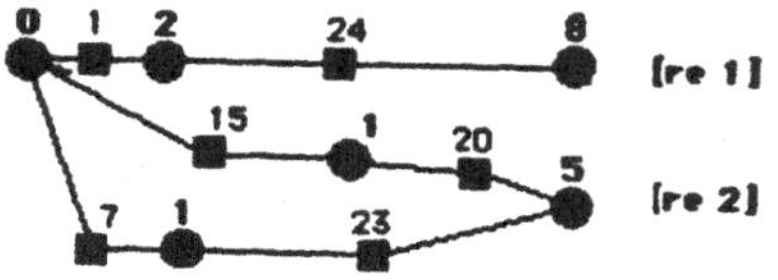

```
0  [*n 'I']        10 [*n 'park']     20 [PP (16 19)]
1  [NP (0)]        11 [NP (9 10)]     21 [NP (11 20)]
2  [*v 'saw']      12 [PP (6 11)]     22 [NP (13 20) (5 23)]
3  [*det 'a']      13 [NP (5 12)]     23 [PP (8 21)]
4  [*n 'man']      14 [VP (2 13)]     24 [VP (2 22)]
5  [NP (3 4)]      15 [S (1 14) (7 12)]
6  [VP (2 5)]      16 [*prep 'with']
7  [S (1 6)]       17 [*det 'a']
8  [*prep 'in']    18 [*n 'scope']
9  [*det 'the']    19 [NP (17 18)]
```

Next Word = '$'

Figure 3-29:  Trace of the Parser (cont.)

After executing "reduce 1", we have figure 3-30.

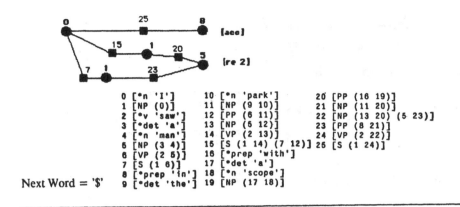

```
        0  [*n 'I']        10  [*n 'park']      20  [PP (16 19)]
        1  [NP (0)]        11  [NP (9 10)]      21  [NP (11 20)]
        2  [*v 'saw']      12  [PP (6 11)]      22  [NP (13 20) (5 23)]
        3  [*det 'a']      13  [NP (5 12)]      23  [PP (8 21)]
        4  [*n 'man']      14  [VP (2 13)]      24  [VP (2 22)]
        5  [NP (3 4)]      15  [S (1 14) (7 12)] 25 [S (1 24)]
        6  [VP (2 5)]      16  [*prep 'with']
        7  [S (1 6)]       17  [*det 'a']
        8  [*prep 'in']    18  [*n 'scope']
Next Word = '$'  9  [*det 'the']  19  [NP (17 18)]
```

Figure 3-30:  Trace of the Parser (cont.)

Then, "reduce 2" is next executed. There are two ways to reduce the stack, and the algorithm would create two new top vertices as shown in figure 3-31.

```
        0  [*n 'I']        10  [*n 'park']      20  [PP (16 19)]
        1  [NP (0)]        11  [NP (9 10)]      21  [NP (11 20)]
        2  [*v 'saw']      12  [PP (6 11)]      22  [NP (13 20) (5 23)]
        3  [*det 'a']      13  [NP (5 12)]      23  [PP (8 21)]
        4  [*n 'man']      14  [VP (2 13)]      24  [VP (2 22)]
        5  [NP (3 4)]      15  [S (1 14) (7 12)] 25 [S (1 24)]
        6  [VP (2 5)]      16  [*prep 'with']   26  [S (15 22)]
        7  [S (1 6)]       17  [*det 'a']       27  [S (7 23)]
        8  [*prep 'in']    18  [*n 'scope']
Next Word = '$'  9  [*det 'the']  19  [NP (17 18)]
```

Figure 3-31:  Trace of the Parser (cont.)

However, those top vertices are combined as one vertex. Furthermore, they represent a local ambiguity because all come immediately from the same state vertex (i.e. the one labeled "0"). Thus, actually, we have figure 3-32.

Finally, the action "accept" is executed. It returns "25" as the top node of the parse forest, and halts the process.

```
      0    25   1
      ●────■────●   [acc]

      0 [*n 'I']        10 [*n 'park']     20 [PP (16 19)]
      1 [NP (0)]        11 [NP (9 10)]     21 [NP (11 20)]
      2 [*v 'saw']      12 [PP (6 11)]     22 [NP (13 20)]
      3 [*det 'a']      13 [NP (6 12)]     23 [PP (8 21)]
      4 [*n 'man']      14 [VP (2 13)]     24 [VP (2 22)]
      5 [NP (3 4)]      15 [S (1 14) (7 12)] 25 [S (1 24) (16 22) (7 23)]
      6 [VP (2 5)]      16 [*prep 'with']
      7 [S (1 6)]       17 [*det 'a']
      8 [*prep 'in']    18 [*n 'scope']
Next Word = '$'  9 [*det 'the']   19 [NP (17 18)]
```

**Figure 3-32:** Trace of the Parser (final)

## 3.3. Managing Multi-part-of-speech Words

This section gives a trace of the algorithm with the sentence "That information is important is doubtful," to demonstrate that our algorithm can handle multi-part-of-speech words (in this sentence, 'that') just like multiple entries without any special mechanism. We use the following grammar and parsing table.

```
-----------------------------------
 (1)    S  --> NP VP
 (2)   NP  --> *det *n
 (3)   NP  --> *n
 (4)   NP  --> *that S
 (5)   VP  --> *be *adj
-----------------------------------
```

Figure 3-33:  Another Example Grammar

| State | *adj | *be | *det | *n | *that | $ | NP | S | VP |
|---|---|---|---|---|---|---|---|---|---|
| 0 | | | sh5 | sh4 | sh3 | | 2 | 1 | |
| 1 | | | | | | acc | | | |
| 2 | | sh6 | | | | | | | 7 |
| 3 | | | sh5 | sh4 | sh3 | | 2 | 8 | |
| 4 | | re3 | | | | | | | |
| 5 | | | | sh9 | | | | | |
| 6 | sh10 | | | | | | | | |
| 7 | | re1 | | | | re1 | | | |
| 8 | | re4 | | | | | | | |
| 9 | | re2 | | | | | | | |
| 10 | | re5 | | | | re5 | | | |

Figure 3-34:  Parsing Table for figure 3-33

At the very beginning, the parse forest contains nothing and the stack contains only one vertex labeled 0. The first word of the sentence is "that", which can be categorized as "*that", "*det" or "*n". The action table tells us that all of these categories are legal. Thus, the algorithm behaves as if a multiple entry is encountered. Three actions, "shift 3", "shift 4" and "shift 5", are to be executed (figure 3-35).

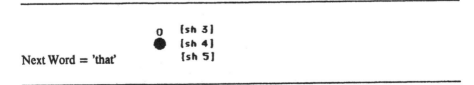

Next Word = 'that'

0  [sh 3]
●  [sh 4]
   [sh 5]

Figure 3-35:  Trace of the Parser

After executing those three shift actions, we have figure 3-36.

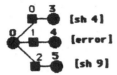

```
0  [*that 'that']
1  [*n 'that']
2  [*det 'that']
```

Next Word = 'information'

**Figure 3-36:** Trace of the Parser (cont.)

Note that three different leaf nodes have been created in the parse forest. One of the three possibilities, "that" as a noun, is discarded immediately after the parser sees the next word "information." After executing the two shift actions, we have figure 3-37.

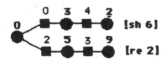

```
0  [*that 'that']
1  [*n 'that']
2  [*det 'that']
3  [*n 'information']
```

Next Word = 'is'

**Figure 3-37:** Trace of the Parser (cont.)

This time, only one leaf node has been created in the parse forest, because both shift actions regarded the word as belonging to the same category, i.e. noun. Now we have two active vertices, and "reduce 3" is arbitrarily chosen as the next action to execute. After executing "reduce 3", we have figure 3-38.

```
0  [*that 'that']
1  [*n 'that']
2  [*det 'that']
3  [*n 'information']
4  [NP (3)]
```

Next Word = 'is'

**Figure 3-38:** Trace of the Parser (cont.)

After executing "reduce 2", we have figure 3-39.

After executing "shift 6", we have figure 3-40.

```
0 [*that 'that']
1 [*n 'that']
2 [*det 'that']
3 [*n 'information']
4 [NP (3)]
5 [NP (2 3)]
```

Next Word = 'is'

Figure 3-39: Trace of the Parser (cont.)

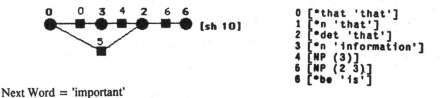

```
0 [*that 'that']
1 [*n 'that']
2 [*det 'that']
3 [*n 'information']
4 [NP (3)]
5 [NP (2 3)]
6 [*be 'is']
```

Next Word = 'important'

Figure 3-40: Trace of the Parser (cont.)

After executing "shift 10", we have figure 3-41.

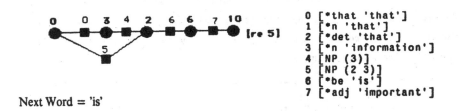

```
0 [*that 'that']
1 [*n 'that']
2 [*det 'that']
3 [*n 'information']
4 [NP (3)]
5 [NP (2 3)]
6 [*be 'is']
7 [*adj 'important']
```

Next Word = 'is'

Figure 3-41: Trace of the Parser (cont.)

After executing "reduce 5", we have figure 3-42.

Now, there are two ways to execute the action "reduce 1". After executing "reduce 1" in both ways, we have figure 3-43.

An error action is finally found for the possibility, "that" as a determiner. After executing "reduce 4", we have figure 3-44.

```
0   0  3  4  2  8  7   [re 1]
                       0 [*that 'that']          8 [VP (6 7)]
           5           1 [*n 'that']
                       2 [*det 'that']
                       3 [*n 'information']
                       4 [NP (3)]
                       5 [NP (2 3)]
                       6 [*be 'is']
Next Word = 'is'       7 [*adj 'important']
```

**Figure 3-42:** Trace of the Parser (cont.)

```
0   0  3  9  8   [re 4]
         !0     1
                [error]
                0 [*that 'that']          8 [VP (6 7)]
                1 [*n 'that']             9 [S (4 8)]
                2 [*det 'that']
                3 [*n 'information']
                4 [NP (3)]
                5 [NP (2 3)]
                6 [*be 'is']
Next Word = 'is'  7 [*adj 'important']
```

**Figure 3-43:** Trace of the Parser (cont.)

```
0  !!  2          0 [*that 'that']          8  [VP (6 7)]
        [sh 6]    1 [*n 'that']             9  [S (4 8)]
                  2 [*det 'that']          10  [S (6 8)]
                  3 [*n 'information']     11  [NP (0 9)]
                  4 [NP (3)]
                  5 [NP (2 3)]
                  6 [*be 'is']
Next Word = 'is'  7 [*adj 'important']
```

**Figure 3-44:** Trace of the Parser (cont.)

After executing "shift 6", and several steps later, we have figure 3-45.

The parser accepts the sentence, and returns "15" as the top node of the parse forest.

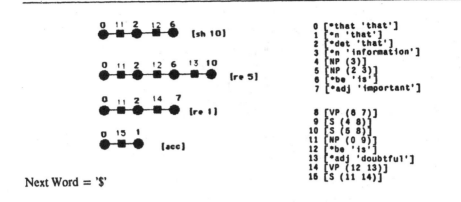

Next Word = '$'

**Figure 3-45:** Trace of the Parser (final)

## 3.4. Managing Unknown Words

In the previous section, we saw the parsing algorithm handling a multi-part-of-speech word just like multiple entries without any special mechanism. That capability can also be applied to handle unknown words (words whose categories are unknown). An unknown word can be thought of as a special type of a multi-part-of-speech word whose categories can be anything. In the following, we present another trace of the parser with the sentence "I * a *", where *'s represent an unknown word. The algorithm can parse more complex sentences such as "I * * *" or even "* * * *", but these examples are perhaps too complex to give their parse traces by hand. We use the same grammar and parsing table as in the first example.

At the very beginning, we have figure 3-46.

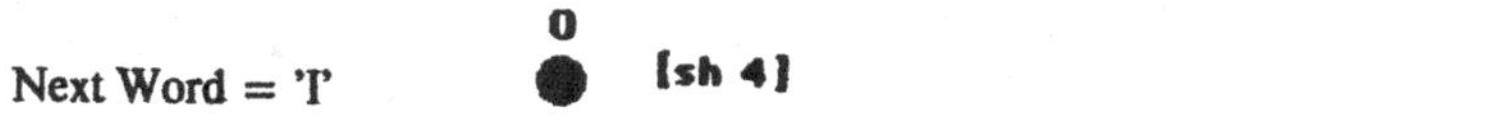

Next Word = 'I'      0      [sh 4]

Figure 3-46:  Trace of the Parser

After executing "shift 4", we have figure 3-47.

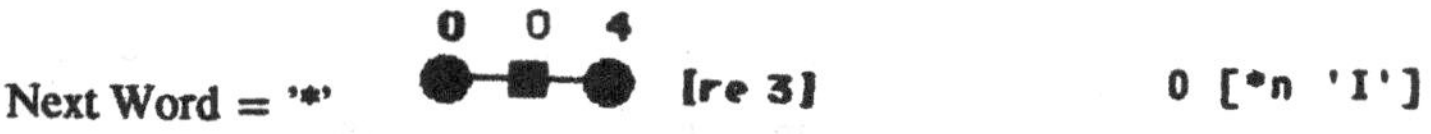

Next Word = '*'      0  0  4   [re 3]          0 [*n 'I']

Figure 3-47:  Trace of the Parser (cont.)

At this point, the parser is looking at the unknown word, "*"; in other words, a word whose categories are *det, *n, *v and *prep. On row 4 of the action table, we have only one kind of action, "reduce 3". Thus the algorithm executes only the action "reduce 3". After executing "reduce 3", we have figure 3-48.

Next Word = '*'      0  1  2   [sh 6]          0 [*n 'I']
                             [sh 7]          1 [NP (0)]

Figure 3-48:  Trace of the Parser (cont.)

On row 2 of the action table, there are two kinds of actions, "shift 6" and "shift 7". This means the unknown word has two possibilities, as a preposition or a verb. After executing both actions, we have figure 3-49.

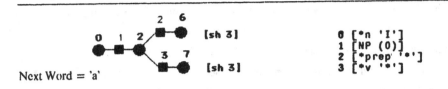

**Figure 3-49:** Trace of the Parser (cont.)

After executing "shift 3" twice, we have figure 3-50.

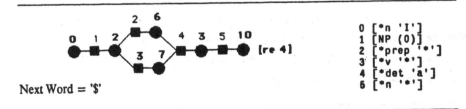

**Figure 3-50:** Trace of the Parser (cont.)

At this point, the parser is again looking at the unknown word, "*". However, since there is only one entry on row 3 in the action table, we can uniquely determine the category of the unknown word, which is a noun. After shifting the unknown word as a noun, we have figure 3-51.

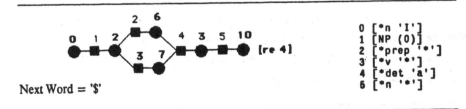

**Figure 3-51:** Trace of the Parser (cont.)

After executing "reduce 4", we have figure 3-52.

After executing both "reduce 6" and "reduce 7", we have figure 3-53.

After executing both "reduce 5" and "reduce 1", we have figure 3-54.

The possibility of the first unknown word being a preposition has now disappeared. The

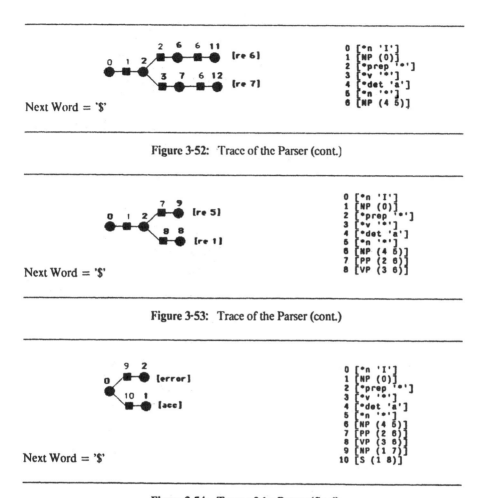

Figure 3-52: Trace of the Parser (cont.)

Figure 3-53: Trace of the Parser (cont.)

Figure 3-54: Trace of the Parser (final)

parser accepts the sentence in only one way, and returns "10" as the root node of the parse forest.

We have shown in this section that our parsing algorithm can handle unknown words without any special mechanism. It might be possible to self-extend the parser's lexical entry by remembering syntactic categories of unknown words [12].

# Chapter 4
# Formal Specification of the Algorithm

---

## 4.1. Introduction

This chapter, which may be omitted without loss of context, presents a more precise specification of the algorithm. Section 4.2 presents a formal specification of the algorithm as a recognizer (i.e. no parse forest is produced), and section 4.3 gives a formal specification of the algorithm as a parser (i.e. a parse forest is produced).

## 4.2. The Recognizer

In this section, we specify our algorithm as a recognizer. Subsection 4.2.1 defines some terms in graph theory. Subsection 4.2.2 then specifies the graph-structured stack. Subsection 4.2.3 gives a specification of our algorithm assuming that its grammar is always LR (i.e. no multiple entries). Since our algorithm is exactly the same as the standard LR algorithm if a grammar is LR, the subsection essentially gives a specification of the standard LR algorithm using our notation for the graph-structured stack. Subsection 4.2.4 gives a specification of our algorithm for non-LR grammars, extending the algorithm given in subsection 4.2.3. This time, however, we assume that a grammar does not contain any e-productions (productions whose right hand side is NIL). Subsection 4.2.5 extends the algorithm in subsection 4.2.4 to handle e-productions. Subsection 4.2.6 finally gives a specification of the full version of our algorithm, refining the algorithm given in subsection 4.2.5. Throughout this chapter, however, the problem of multi-part-of-speech words and unknown words are disregarded, and we assume that each input word has at most one grammatical category.

### 4.2.1. Terms in Graph Theory

A *Directed graph* is a pair $\langle V, E\rangle$, where $V$ is a set of elements called *vertices* and $E$ is a relation on $V$.

A pair $\langle v, w\rangle \in E$ is called an *edge from v to w*.

If $\langle v, w\rangle$ is an edge we say that $v$ is a *predecessor* of $w$ and $w$ is a *successor* of $v$.

SUCCESSORS($v$) is a function that takes a vertex $v$ as its argument and returns a set of all vertices whose predecessor is $v$.

A sequence of vertices $(v_0\ v_1\ ....,\ v_n)$ is a *path of length n* from vertex $v_0$ to vertex $v_n$ if there is an edge from vertex $v_{i-1}$ to vertex $v_i$ for $1 \le i \le n$. A sequence of vertices $(v_0\ v_1\ ....,\ v_n)$ is also denoted as $(v_n \leftarrow v_{n-1} \leftarrow .... \leftarrow v_0)$.

A *cycle* is a path $(v_0\ v_1\ ....,\ v_n)$ in which $v_0 = v_n$.

The *in-degree* of a vertex $v$ is the number of edges to $v$, and the *out-degree* of $v$ is the number of edges from $v$.

A vertex having in-degree 0 will be called a *top* vertex (also called a *root*. One having out-degree 0 is called a *leaf*.

A *directed acyclic graph* is a directed graph that has no cycles.

### 4.2.2. The Graph-Structured Stack

This subsection specifies the graph-structured stack informally described in subsection 2.3.3.

A *graph-structured stack* $\Gamma$ is a directed acyclic graph, which has only one leaf vertex, $v_0$, labeled with the state number 0. The special vertex $v_0$ is called the *bottom* of $\Gamma$.

All vertices whose distance from $v_0$ is an even number ($2*n$, where n is positive integer) are called *state vertices*, and they are labeled with a state number. All vertices whose distance from $v_0$ is an odd number are called *symbol vertices*, and they are labeled with a grammar symbol.

We denote a state vertex with a circle and a symbol vertex with a square. Also, state vertices are usually represented by variables $v$, $w$ and $u$, while symbol vertices are represented by variables $x$, $y$ and $z$.

STATE($v$) is a function that takes a state vertex as its argument and returns the state number which is labeled on the vertex. SYMBOL($x$) is a function that takes a symbol vertex as its argument and returns the symbol which is labeled on the vertex.

### 4.2.3. The algorithm for LR grammars

Before giving a formal specification of our algorithm, we first give a formal specification of the standard LR parsing algorithm with our notation in order to provide the reader with a helpful introduction to the following subsections. The purpose of this subsection is not to specify standard LR parsing, but rather to help the reader understand the specification of our algorithm better. Therefore, some of the definitions and parts of the algorithm in the following specification are somewhat redundant or unnecessarily complicated for standard LR parsing, but will be required when we present our algorithm. The figure 4-1 presents the pre-defined functions and global variables essential to understanding our algorithm.

PARSE(G, $a_1....a_n$)

- $\Gamma \Leftarrow \phi$
- $a_{n+1} \Leftarrow$ '$'
- $r \Leftarrow$ FALSE
- create in $\Gamma$ a vertex $v_0$ labeled $s_0$.
- $A \Leftarrow \{v_0\}$
- **for** $i \Leftarrow 0$ **to** n **do** PARSEWORD($i$).
- **return** $r$.

PARSEWORD($i$)

- $R, Q \Leftarrow \phi$.
- **repeat**
  - **if** $A \neq \phi$ **then do** ACTOR.
  - **elseif** $R \neq \phi$ **then do** REDUCER.
- **until** $R = \phi \wedge A = \phi$.
- **do** SHIFTER

| | |
|---|---|
| **G** | Grammar; i.e. a set of productions. |
| $a_1....a_n$ | Input string with the length of n. |
| **Γ** | The graph-structured stack. |
| LEFT(p) | The left hand side symbol of production p. |
| \|p\| | The length of the right hand side of production p. |
| STATE(v) | Takes a vertex in Γ as its argument, and returns a state number labeled with the vertex. |
| SYMBOL(x) | Takes a vertex in Γ as its argument, and returns a symbol labeled with the vertex. |
| SUCCESSORS(v) | Takes a vertex in Γ as its argument, and returns a set of all vertices in Γ such that there is an edge from v to each of these vertices. |
| GOTO(s, N) | Look up the goto table. s is a state number and N is a non-terminal. Returns a state number. |
| ACTION(s, a) | Look up the action table. s is a state number and a is a terminal symbol. Returns an action; 'accept', 'shift s', 'reduce p' or 'error'. |
| r | Contains the result. If r=TRUE then the sentence is accepted , else the sentence is rejected. It is altered in ACTOR, and initialized in PARSE. |
| A | A set of active vertices of Γ to be processed. ACTOR will take care of it. It is also altered in SHIFTER and REDUCER, and initialized in PARSE. In standard LR parsing, the number of its elements is no more than one at anytime. |
| R | A set of paths to be reduced. In standard LR parsing, the number of its elements is no more than one. An element is a 2-tuple ⟨v, p⟩, where v is a starting vertex of the path to be reduced and p is a production. The existence of ⟨v, p⟩ in R means that 'reduce p' is to be applied on the path starting with the vertex v. REDUCER will take care of it. It is also altered in ACTOR, and initialized in PARSEWORD. |
| Q | A set of vertices to be shifted on. In standard LR parsing, the number of its elements is no more than one. An element is a 2-tuple ⟨v, s⟩, where v is the vertex to be shifted on and s is a state number. The existence of ⟨v, s⟩ in Q means that 'shift s' is to be applied on v. SHIFTER will take care of them. It is also altered in ACTOR, and initialized in PARSEWORD. |

**Table 4-1:** Pre-defined functions and global variables

ACTOR

- remove one element $v$ from $A$.
- $\alpha \Leftarrow$ ACTION(STATE($v$), $a_{i+1}$)
- **if** $\alpha$ = 'accept' **then** $r \Leftarrow$ TRUE.
- **if** $\alpha$ = 'shift $s$' **then** add $\langle v, s \rangle$ to $Q$.
- **if** $\alpha$ = 'reduce $p$' **then** add $\langle v, p \rangle$ to $R$.

REDUCER

- remove an element $\langle v, p \rangle$ from $R$.
- $N \Leftarrow$ LEFT($p$).
- Let $w$ be a vertex whose distance from $v$ is $2 * |p|$.
- $s \Leftarrow$ GOTO(STATE($w$, N)).
- create in $\Gamma$ two vertices $u$ and $x$ labeled $s$ and N, respectively.
- create two edges in $\Gamma$ from $u$ to $x$ and from $x$ to $w$.
- $A \Leftarrow \{u\}$.

SHIFTER

- remove an element $\langle v, s \rangle$ from $Q$.
- create in $\Gamma$ two vertices $w$ and $x$, labeled $s$ and $a_{i+1}$.
- create edges in $\Gamma$ from $w$ to $x$ and $x$ to $v$.
- $A \Leftarrow \{w\}$.

The examples of applying REDUCER and SHIFTER are shown below. In the REDUCER example above, we assumed GOTO(1,D)=4. We do not really 'pop' away items from a stack; we leave the items and mark them 'inactive', as shown in the above example. SHIFTER, on the other hand, behaves much like a normal stack, as shown in the following example.

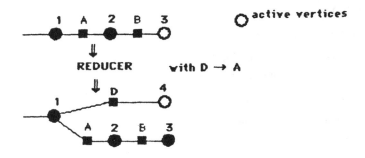

Figure 4-1:  Example of REDUCER

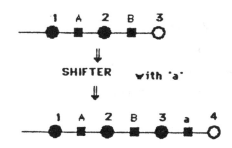

Figure 4-2:  Example of SHIFTER

### 4.2.4. The algorithm for non-e grammars

We now extend the specification in the preceding subsection to handle multiple entries. We still assume in this subsection, however, that no e-production is included in a grammar. In the following subsection, we then extend the specification so that the algorithm handles e-productions as well.

The fundamental difference between the algorithm in subsection 4.2.3 and our algorithm is that in ours the ACTION function may return more than one action due to the existence of multiple entries. This implies that more than one action may be processed by ACTOR. ACTOR may put more than one element to $R$, and all those elements are processed by REDUCER, causing the existence of more than one active vertex at the same time. If two or more active vertices exist, an input symbol may be shifted more than once; when SHIFTER is executed, there may be more than one element in $Q$. For these reasons, set variables $A$, $R$

and $Q$ were used in the last subsection despite the fact that at most only one element could exist in each set.

To make the specification clearer, we can classify a set of state vertices in $\Gamma$ into $n+1$ subclasses, $U_0, ..., U_n$, depending on when a vertex was created. Each subclass, $U_i$ is a set of state vertices which were created while parsing $a_i$. A typical graph-structured stack is shown below as an example.

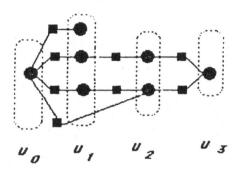

**Figure 4-3:** The Graph-Structured Stack

Table 4-2 presents the pre-defined functions and global variables necessary to specify the algorithm.

PARSE(G, $a_1....a_n$)

- $\Gamma \Leftarrow \phi$
- $a_{n+1} \Leftarrow$ '$' 
- $r \Leftarrow$ FALSE
- create in $\Gamma$ a vertex $v_0$ labeled $s_0$.
- $U_0 \Leftarrow \{v_0\}$
- **for** $i \Leftarrow 0$ **to** n **do** PARSEWORD($i$).
- **return** $r$.

| | |
|---|---|
| ACTION($s$, a) | Look up the action table. $s$ is a state number and a is a terminal symbol. Returns a list of actions. |
| $U_i$ | A set of vertices in $\Gamma$ which were created when parsing $a_i$. Let $a_i$ be the word most recently shifted. Then, $U_i$ is a set of top vertices. It is altered in PARSE, REDUCER and SHIFTER. |
| $A$ | A set of active vertices in $U_i$ to be processed. ACTOR will take care of them. It is also altered in REDUCER, and initialized in PARSEWORD. |
| $R$ | A set of top edges to be reduced. Each element is a 3-tuple $\langle v, x, p \rangle$, where $v \in U_i$, $x \in$ SUCCESSORS($v$) and $p$ is a production rule. The existence of $\langle v, x, p \rangle$ in $R$ means that 'reduce $p$' is to be applied on all paths starting with the edge $(v, x)$. REDUCER will take care of them. It is also altered in ACTOR, and initialized in PARSEWORD. |
| $Q$ | A set of vertices to be shifted. Each element is a 2-tuple $\langle v, s \rangle$, where $v \in U_i$ and $s$ is a state number. The existence of $\langle v, s \rangle$ in $Q$ means that 'shift $s$' is to be applied on $v$. SHIFTER will take care of them. It is also altered in ACTOR, and initialized in PARSEWORD. |

Table 4-2: Pre-defined functions and global variables

PARSEWORD($i$)

- $A \Leftarrow U_i$.
- $R, Q \Leftarrow \phi$.
- **repeat**
  - **if** $A \neq \phi$ **then do** ACTOR.
  - **elseif** $R \neq \phi$ **then do** REDUCER.
- **until** $R = \phi \wedge A = \phi$.
- **do** SHIFTER.

ACTOR

- remove one element $v$ from $A$.
- **for all** $\alpha \in$ ACTION(STATE($v$), $a_{i+1}$) **do**
    - ○ **if** $\alpha$ = 'accept' **then** $r \Leftarrow$ TRUE.
    - ○ **if** $\alpha$ = 'shift $s$' **then** add $\langle v, s \rangle$ to $Q$.
    - ○ **if** $\alpha$ = 'reduce $p$' **then**
        - **for all** $x$ such that $x \in$ SUCCESSORS($v$), add $\langle v, x, p \rangle$ to $R$.

REDUCER

- remove one element $\langle v, x, p \rangle$ from $R$.
- $N \Leftarrow$ LEFT($p$)
- **for all** $w$ such that there exists a path of length $2*|p|$-1 from $x$ to $w$ **do**
    - ○ $s \Leftarrow$ GOTO(STATE($w$), N)
    - ○ **if** there exists $u$ such that $u \in U_i \wedge$ STATE($u$) = $s$ **then**
        - if there already exists a path of length 2 from $u$ to $w$ **then**
            - ○ do nothing.
        - **else**
            - ○ create in $\Gamma$ a vertex $z$ labeled N.
            - ○ create two edges in $\Gamma$ from $u$ to $z$ and from $z$ to $w$.
            - ○ **if** $u \notin A$ **then**
                - **for all** $q$ such that 'reduce $q$' $\in$ ACTION(STATE($u$), $a_{i+1}$) do add $\langle u, z, q \rangle$ to $R$.
    - ○ **else** /* if there doesn't exist $u$ such that $u \in U_i \wedge$ STATE($u$) = $s$ */
        - create in $\Gamma$ two vertices $u$ and $z$ labeled $s$ and N, respectively.
        - create two edges in $\Gamma$ from $u$ to $z$ and from $z$ to $w$.
        - add $u$ to both $A$ and $U_i$.

SHIFTER

- **for all** $s$ such that $\exists\, v (\langle v, s \rangle \in Q)$,

  o create in $\Gamma$ a vertex $w$ labeled $s$.

  o add $w$ to $U_{i+1}$.

  o **for all** $v$ such that $\langle v, s \rangle \in Q$ **do**

    - create $x$ labeled $a_{i+1}$ in $\Gamma$.

    - create edges in $\Gamma$ from $w$ to $x$ and from $x$ to $v$.

### 4.2.5. The algorithm for e-grammars

In this subsection, we extend the algorithm in the preceding subsection to handle e-productions (productions whose right hand side is empty). Because of the allowance of e-productions, there may be an arbitrary number of e-symbols between every adjunct pair of input symbols. The number of the e-symbols is, however, always finite, as we assumed in the preceding sections. Our algorithm will perform as if there were an appropriate number of e's as normal input symbols between every adjunct pair of input symbols. Thus, an input string $a_1....a_n$ can be thought of as the following:

$$e...e\; a_1\; e...e\; a_2 . . . . . . . a_n\; e...e\; \$$$

---

| | |
|---|---|
| $U_{i,j}$ | A set of vertices in $\Gamma$ which were created when parsing $a_i$, if $j=0$, or the $j$-th e after $a_i$ if $j \geq 1$. It is altered in PARSE, ACTOR, REDUCER and SHIFTER. |
| $R_e$ | A set of vertices to be reduced by an e-production. Each element is a 2-tuple $\langle v, p \rangle$, where $v \in U_{i,j}$ and $p$ is an e-production. The existence of $\langle v, p \rangle$ in $R_e$ means that 'reduce $p$' is to be applied on the vertex $v$. E-REDUCER will take care of them. It is also altered in ACTOR, and initialized in PARSEWORD. |
| $Q$ | A set of vertices to be shifted. Each element is a 2-tuple $\langle v, s \rangle$, where $v \in U_{i,0} \cup U_{i,1} \cup ... \cup U_{i,j}$ and $s$ is a state number. The existence of $\langle v, s \rangle$ in $Q$ means that 'shift $s$' is to be applied on $v$. SHIFTER will take care of them. It is also altered in ACTOR, and initialized in PARSEWORD. |

---

**Table 4-3:** Global variables

PARSE(G, $a_1....a_n$)

- $\Gamma \Leftarrow \phi$
- $a_{n+1} \Leftarrow$ '$' 
- $r \Leftarrow$ FALSE
- create in $\Gamma$ a vertex $v_0$ labeled $s_0$.
- $U_{0,0} \Leftarrow \{v_0\}$
- **for** $i \Leftarrow 0$ **to** n **do** PARSEWORD($i$).
- **return** $r$.


PARSEWORD($i$)

- $j \Leftarrow 0$.
- $A \Leftarrow U_{i,0}$.
- $R, Q, R_e \Leftarrow \phi$.
- **repeat**
    - ○ **if** $A \neq \phi$ **then do** ACTOR
    - ○ **elseif** $R \neq \phi$ **then do** REDUCER
    - ○ **elseif** $R_e \neq \phi$ **then do** E-REDUCER
- **until** $A = \phi \wedge R = \phi \wedge R_e = \phi$.
- **do** SHIFTER.

## ACTOR

- remove one element $v$ from $A$.
- **for all** $\alpha \in$ ACTION(STATE($v$), $a_{i+1}$) **do**
  - ○ **if** $\alpha =$ 'accept' **then** $r \Leftarrow$ TRUE.
  - ○ **if** $\alpha =$ 'shift $s$' **then** add $\langle v, s \rangle$ to $Q$.
  - ○ **if** $\alpha =$ 'reduce $p$' and $p$ is not an e-production **then**
    - **for all** $x$ such that $x \in$ SUCCESSORS($v$), add $\langle v, x, p \rangle$ to $R$.
  - ○ **if** $\alpha =$ 'reduce $p$' and $p$ is an e-production **then** add $\langle v, p \rangle$ to $R_e$.


## REDUCER

- remove one element $\langle v, x, p \rangle$ from $R$.
- $N \Leftarrow$ LEFT($p$)
- **for all** $w$ such that there exists a path of length $2*|p|-1$ from $x$ to $w$ **do**
  - ○ $s \Leftarrow$ GOTO(STATE($w$), N)
  - ○ **if** there exists $u$ such that $u \in U_{i,j} \wedge$ STATE($u$) = $s$ **then**
    - if there already exists a path of length 2 from $u$ to $w$ **then**
      - ○ do nothing.
    - **else**
      - ○ create in $\Gamma$ a vertex $z$ labeled N.
      - ○ create two edges in $\Gamma$ from $u$ to $z$ and from $z$ to $w$.
      - ○ **if** $u \notin A$ **then**
        - **for all** $q$ such that 'reduce $q$' $\in$ ACTION(STATE($u$), $a_{i+1}$) **do** add $\langle u, z, q \rangle$ to $R$.
  - ○ **else** /* if there doesn't exist $u$ such that $u \in U_{i,j} \wedge$ STATE($u$) = $s$ */
    - create in $\Gamma$ two vertices $u$ and $z$ labeled $s$ and N, respectively.
    - create two edges in $\Gamma$ from $u$ to $z$ and from $z$ to $w$.
    - add $u$ to both $A$ and $U_{i,j}$.

E-REDUCER

- $U_{i,j+1} \Leftarrow \phi$
- **for all** $\langle v, p \rangle \in R_e$ **do**
  - ○ N $\Leftarrow$ LEFT($p$).
  - ○ $s \Leftarrow$ GOTO($v$, N).
  - ○ **if** there exists $w$ such that $w \in U_{i,j+1} \wedge$ STATE($w$) = $s$ **then**
    - • create in $\Gamma$ a vertex $x$ labeled N.
    - • create edges in $\Gamma$ from $w$ to $x$ and from $x$ to $v$.
  - ○ **else**
    - • create in $\Gamma$ vertices $w$ and $x$ labeled $s$ and N.
    - • create edges in $\Gamma$ from $w$ to $x$ and from $x$ to $v$.
    - • add $w$ to $U_{i,j+1}$.
- $R_e \Leftarrow \phi$.
- $A \Leftarrow U_{i,j+1}$.
- $j \Leftarrow j+1$.


SHIFTER

- $U_{i+1,0} \Leftarrow \phi$.
- **for all** $s$ such that $\exists\, v\, (\langle v, s \rangle \in Q)$,
  - ○ create in $\Gamma$ a vertex $w$ labeled $s$.
  - ○ add $w$ to $U_{i+1,0}$.
  - ○ **for all** $v$ such that $\langle v, s \rangle \in Q$ **do**
    - • create $x$ labeled $a_{i+1}$ in $\Gamma$.
    - • create edges in $\Gamma$ from $w$ to $x$ and from $x$ to $v$.

#### 4.2.6. The full version of the algorithm

In this subsection, we give a specification of the full version of our algorithm, making one refinement on the algorithm in subsection 4.2.5. The algorithm in subsection 4.2.5 may produce a graph-structured stack which looks like:

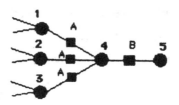

Figure 4-4:  Example before Refinement

This graph-structured stack could be more efficiently represented as in figure 4-5.

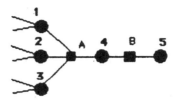

Figure 4-5:  Example after Refinement

This refinement is crucial particularly when we extend our recognition algorithm to a parsing algorithm; it is not merely to save space for graph-structured stack representation. Suppose ACTION(5, a) includes 'reduce $p$' where $p$ is C → AB and a is whatever symbol the algorithm is looking at as a lookahead.    Suppose also GOTO(1, C)=GOTO(2, C)=GOTO(3, C)=6. The first representation must reduce AB into C three times and apply the GOTO function three times, producing the graph-structured stack in figure 4-6. On the other hand, the second representation must apply the GOTO function three times, but it must reduce AB into C only once, producing the graph-structured stack in figure 4-7. To achieve this refinement, we modify REDUCER, E-REDUCER and SHIFTER.

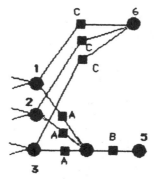

**Figure 4-6:** Another Example before Refinement

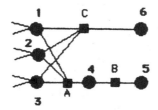

**Figure 4-7:** Another Example after Refinement

PARSE(G, $a_1....a_n$)

++ Same as subsection 4.2.5 ++


PARSEWORD(*i*)

++ Same as subsection 4.2.5 ++


ACTOR

++ Same as subsection 4.2.5 ++

REDUCER

- remove one element $\langle v, x, p\rangle$ from $R$.

- $N \Leftarrow \text{LEFT}(p)$

- **for all** $y$ such that there exists a path of length $2*|p|-2$ from $x$ to $y$ **do**

  o **for all** $s$ such that $\exists w (w \in \text{SUCCESSORS}(y) \land \text{GOTO}(\text{STATE}(w), N) = s)$ **do**

    - $W \Leftarrow \{w | w \in \text{SUCCESSORS}(y) \land \text{GOTO}(\text{STATE}(w), N) = s\}$

    - **if** there exists $u$ such that $u \in U_{i,j} \land \text{STATE}(u) = s$ **then**

      o **if** there already exists an edge from $u$ to a vertex $z$ such that $\text{SUCCESSORS}(z) = W$ **then** do nothing.

      o **else**

        - create in $\Gamma$ a vertex $z$ labeled N.

        - create an edge·in $\Gamma$ from $u$ to $z$.

        - **for all** $w \in W$ **do**

          o create an edge in $\Gamma$ from $z$ to $w$.

        - **if** $u \notin A$ **then**

          o **for all** $q$ such that 'reduce $q$' $\in$ $\text{ACTION}(\text{STATE}(u), a_{i+1})$ and $|q|$ is not 0 **do**

            - add $\langle u, z, q\rangle$ to $R$

    - **else**

      o create in $\Gamma$ two vertices $u$ and $z$ labeled $s$ and N.

      o create in $\dot{\Gamma}$ an edge from $u$ to $z$.

      o **for all** $w \in W$ **do**

        - create in $\Gamma$ an edge from $z$ to $w$.

      o add $u$ to both $A$ and $U_{i,j}$.

E-REDUCER

- $U_{i,j+1} \Leftarrow \phi$
- **for all** $s$ such that $\exists \langle v, p \rangle \in R_e$ such that GOTO(STATE($v$), LEFT($p$)) $= s$
  **do**

  - $N \Leftarrow$ LEFT($p$).
  - create in $\Gamma$ vertices $w$ and $x$ labeled $s$ and N, respectively.
  - create in $\Gamma$ an edge from $w$ to $x$.
  - add $w$ to $U_{i,j+1}$.
  - **for all** $\langle v, p \rangle \in R_e$ such that GOTO(STATE($v$), LEFT($p$)) $= s$ **do**
    - create in $\Gamma$ an edge from $x$ to $v$.
- $R_e \Leftarrow \phi$.
- $A \Leftarrow U_{i,j+1}$.
- $j \Leftarrow j+1$.


SHIFTER

- $U_{i+1,0} \Leftarrow \phi$.
- **for all** $s$ such that $\exists v (\langle v, s \rangle \in Q)$,

  - create in $\Gamma$ vertices $x$ and $w$ labeled $s$ and $a_{i+1}$, respectively.
  - create in $\Gamma$ an edge from $w$ to $x$.
  - add $w$ to $U_{i+1,0}$.
  - **for all** $v$ such that $\langle v, s \rangle \in Q$ **do**
    - create an edge in $\Gamma$ from $x$ to $v$.

## 4.3. The Parser

This section extends the formal specification of the recognition algorithm in the last section into that of the parsing algorithm (i.e. a parse forest is produced). Subsection 4.3.1 defines some additional preliminary terms in graph theory. Subsection 4.3.2 defines the parse forest as well as several utility functions. Finally, subsection 4.3.3 gives a formal specification of our parsing algorithm.

### 4.3.1. Additional Terms in Graph Theory

An *ordered directed graph* is a pair $\langle V, E \rangle$ where $V$ is a set of vertices and $E$ is a set of linearly ordered lists of edges. Each element of $E$ is a 2-tuple $\langle v, (w_1, w_2, ..., w_n) \rangle$, where $v$, $w_i$ $\in V$. This element would indicate that, for vertex $v$, there are n edges leaving $v$, the first going to $w_1$, the second going to $w_2$, and so forth. We call $(w_1, w_2, ..., w_n)$ a *successor list* of vertex $v$.

In a normal ordered directed graph, there is at most one successor list for each vertex in $V$. That is, for every pair of elements in $E \langle v, L \rangle$ and $\langle v', L \rangle$, $v \neq v'$.

### 4.3.2. The parse forest

The *shared-packed forest* T is an acyclic ordered directed graph $(V, E)$ in which each vertex may have more than one successor list. That is, in a shared-packed forest, there may be more than one element in $E$, $\langle v, L \rangle, \langle v', L \rangle, \langle v'', L'' \rangle, ...$ such that $v = v' = v'' = ....$.

SUBNODES($v$) is a function which takes a vertex $v$ in $V$ as its argument and returns a set of successor lists $\{L_1, L_2, ...\}$ such that $\langle v, L_i \rangle \in E$ for all i.

ADDSUBNODE is a function that takes a vertex $v$ in T and a list of successors as its arguments, and returns NIL. As its side effect, it adds $\langle v, L \rangle$ to $E$ in $T = \langle V, E \rangle$. Suppose SUBNODES($v$) $\equiv \{(w_1, w_2)(w_3, w_4)\}$. After applying ADDSUBNODE($v$, $(w_5, w_6)$), SUBNODES($v$) will be $\{(w_1, w_2)(w_3, w_4) (w_5, w_6)\}$.

### 4.3.3. The parsing algorithm

This subsection finally presents a formal specification of our complete parsing algorithm.

---

| | |
|---|---|
| **T** | The parse forest. |
| SUBNODES($v$) | Takes a vertex $v$ in T as its argument, and returns a set of successor lists, $\{L_1, L_2, ...\}$ such that $\langle v, L_i \rangle \in E$ for all i. |
| ADDSUBNODE($v$, $L$) | Adds a successor list $\langle v, L \rangle$ to $E$ in T $= (V, E)$. |

---

**Table 4-4:** Pre-defined functions and global variables

PARSE(G, $a_1$....$a_n$)

- $\Gamma \Leftarrow \phi$
- $T \Leftarrow \phi$
- $r \Leftarrow$ NIL
- $a_{n+1} \Leftarrow$ '$'
- create in $\Gamma$ a vertex $v_0$ labeled $s_0$.
- $U_{0,0} \Leftarrow \{v_0\}$
- **for** $i \Leftarrow 0$ **to** n **do** PARSEWORD($i$).
- **return** $r$, as the root of the parse forest.

PARSEWORD($i$)

- $j \Leftarrow 0$.
- $A \Leftarrow U_{i,0}$.
- $R, Q, R_c \Leftarrow \phi$.
- **repeat**
  - ○ **if** $A \neq \phi$ **then do** ACTOR
  - ○ **elseif** $R \neq \phi$ **then do** REDUCER
  - ○ **elseif** $R_e \neq \phi$ **then do** E-REDUCER
- **until** $A = \phi \wedge R = \phi \wedge R_e = \phi$.
- **do** SHIFTER.

ACTOR

- remove one element $v$ from $A$.
- **for all** $\alpha \in$ ACTION(STATE($v$), $a_{i+1}$) **do**
  - ○ **if** $\alpha =$ 'accept' **then** $r \Leftarrow v$.
  - ○ **if** $\alpha =$ 'shift $s$' **then** add $\langle v, s \rangle$ to $Q$.
  - ○ **if** $\alpha =$ 'reduce $p$' and $p$ is not an e-production **then**
    - **for all** $x$ such that $x \in$ SUCCESSORS($v$), add $\langle v, x, p \rangle$ to $R$.
  - ○ **if** $\alpha =$ 'reduce $p$' and $p$ is an e-production **then** add $\langle v, p \rangle$ to $R_e$.

REDUCER

- remove one element $\langle v, x, p \rangle$ from $R$.

- $N \Leftarrow \text{LEFT}(p)$

- **for all** $y$ such that there exists a path of length $2*|p|-2$ from $x$ to $y$ **do**

  o $L \Leftarrow (\text{SYMBOL}(z_1), \text{SYMBOL}(z_2), ...., \text{SYMBOL}(z_{|p|}))$, where $z_1 = x$, $z_{|p|} = y$ and $z_2...z_{|p|-1}$ are symbol vertices in the path from $x$ to $y$.

  o **for all** $s$ such that $\exists w (w \in \text{SUCCESSORS}(y) \wedge \text{GOTO}(\text{STATE}(w), N) = s)$ **do**

    - $W \Leftarrow \{w | w \in \text{SUCCESSORS}(y) \wedge \text{GOTO}(\text{STATE}(w), N) = s\}$

    - **if** there exists $u$ such that $u \in U_{i,j} \wedge \text{STATE}(u) = s$ **then**

      o **if** there already exists an edge from $u$ to a vertex $z$ such that $\text{SUCCESSORS}(z) = W$ **then** ADDSUBNODE(SYMBOL($z$), $L$).

    o **else**

      - create a vertex $n$ in T labeled N.

      - ADDSUBNODE($n$, $L$).

      - create in $\Gamma$ a vertex $z$ labeled $n$.

      - create an edge in $\Gamma$ from $u$ to $z$.

      - **for all** $w \in W$ **do**

        o create an edge in $\Gamma$ from $z$ to $w$.

      - **if** $u \notin A$ **then**

        o **for all** $q$ such that 'reduce $q$' $\in$ ACTION(STATE($u$), $a_{i+1}$) and $|q|$ is not 0 **do**

          - add $\langle u, z, q \rangle$ to $R$

- **else**

  o create in T a vertex $n$ labeled N.

  o ADDSUBNODE($n$, $L$).

  o create in $\Gamma$ two vertices $u$ and $z$ labeled $s$ and $n$.

  o create in $\Gamma$ an edge from $u$ to $z$.

  o **for all** $w \in W$ **do**

    - create in $\Gamma$ an edge from $z$ to $w$.

o add $u$ to both $A$ and $U_{i,j}$.

E-REDUCER

- $U_{i,j+1} \Leftarrow \phi$
- **for all** $s$ such that $\exists \langle v, p \rangle \in R_e$ such that GOTO(STATE($v$), LEFT($p$)) $= s$ **do**

  o $N \Leftarrow$ LEFT($p$).

  o create in T a vertex $n$ labeled N.

  o ADDSUBNODE($n$, NIL).

  o create in $\Gamma$ vertices $w$ and $x$ labeled $s$ and $n$, respectively.

  o create in $\Gamma$ an edge from $w$ to $x$.

  o add $w$ to $U_{i,j+1}$.

  o **for all** $\langle v, p \rangle \in R_e$ such that GOTO(STATE($v$), LEFT($p$)) $= s$ **do**

    • create in $\Gamma$ an edge from $x$ to $v$.

- $R_e \Leftarrow \phi$.
- $A \Leftarrow U_{i,j+1}$.
- $j \Leftarrow j+1$.

SHIFTER

- $U_{i+1,0} \Leftarrow \phi$.
- create in T a vertex $n$ labeled $a_{i+1}$.
- **for all** $s$ such that $\exists\, v\, (\langle v, s \rangle \in Q)$,

  o create in $\Gamma$ vertices $x$ and $w$ labeled $s$ and $n$, respectively.

  o create in $\Gamma$ an edge from $w$ to $x$.

  o add $w$ to $U_{i+1,0}$.

  o **for all** $v$ such that $\langle v, s \rangle \in Q$ **do**

    • create an edge in $\Gamma$ from $x$ to $v$.

## 4.4. Summary

We have presented a formal specification of our parsing algorithm. A specification of the LR table construction algorithm can be found in appendix A.

# Chapter 5
# Comparison with Other Algorithms

---

## 5.1. Introduction

There have been several general parsing algorithms that run in polynomial time. Theoretically speaking, the fastest algorithm at present is Valiant's algorithm. Valiant [55] reduced the context-free parsing problem to the Boolean Matrix Multiplication problem [22], and his algorithm runs in time $O(n^{2.81})$. This algorithm is, however, of only theoretical interest, because the coefficient of $n^{2.81}$ is so large that the algorithm runs faster than conventional $n^3$ algorithms only when an input sentence is tremendously long. Practically speaking, on the other hand, the most well-known parsing algorithm is Earley's algorithm [21, 20, 1, 25], which runs in time $O(n^3)$. This book compares our algorithm mainly with this algorithm.

All other practical algorithms seem to bear some similarity with or relation to Earley's algorithm. Another algorithm which is as well-known as Earley's algorithm is the Cocke-Younger-Kasami (CYK) algorithm [59, 25, 1]. Graham *et al.* [26], however, revealed that the CYK algorithm is "almost" identical to Earley's algorithm, by giving an improved version of the CYK algorithm which is very similar to Earley's algorithm. The *chart parsing algorithm* is basically the same as the CYK algorithm. The *active chart parsing algorithm* is basically the same as Earley's algorithm, although it does not necessarily have to parse from left to right. Bouckaert *et al.* [8] extended Earley's algorithm to perform tests similar to those introduced in LL and LR algorithms. *Improved nodal span* [17] and LINGOL [43] are also similar to Earley's algorithm, but both of them require grammars to be in Chomsky Normal Form (CNF).

These all practical general parsing algorithms seem to be like Earley's algorithm, in that they employ the tabular parsing method; they all construct *well-formed substring tables* [46]. In chart parsing, such tables are called *charts*. The representation of one well-formed

71

substring is called an "edge" in active chart parsing, a "state" in Earley's algorithm, a "dotted rule" in Graham's algorithm and an "item" in Aho and Ullman [1]. Throughout this book, we call a well-formed substring an *item*.

## 5.2. Recognition time

No existing general parsing algorithm utilizes LR parsing tables. All of the practical algorithms mentioned above construct *sets of items* by adding an item to a set, one by one, during parsing. Our algorithm, on the other hand, is sufficiently different; it precomputes sets of items in advance during the time of parsing table construction, and maintains pointers (i.e., state numbers) to the precomputed sets of items, rather than maintaining the items themselves.

Because of this major difference, our algorithm has the following three properties.

- It is more efficient, if a grammar is "close" to LR: that is, if its LR parsing table contains relatively few multiple entries. In general, less ambiguous grammars tend to have fewer multiple entries in their parsing table. In an extreme case, if a grammar is LR, our algorithm is as efficient as an LR parsing algorithm, except for minor overheads.

- It is less efficient, if a grammar is "densely" ambiguous as in figure 5-1. This kind of grammar tends to have many multiple entries in its LR parsing table. Our algorithm may take more than $O(n^3)$ time with "densely" ambiguous grammars.

```
S --> S S S S
S --> S S S
S --> S S
S --> x
```

```
sentence = 'xxxxxx'
```

**Figure 5-1:** Heavy Ambiguity

- It is not able to handle infinitely ambiguous grammars and cyclic grammars[6] (figure 5-2 and 5-3), although it can handle e-grammars and left-recursive grammars. If a grammar is cyclic, our algorithm never terminates. The existing general parsing algorithms can parse those sentences (figure 5-1, 5-2 and 5-3) still in time proportional to $n^3$.

It is certain that no natural language grammars have infinite ambiguity or cyclic rules. It is

---

[6]Those two kinds of grammars are equivalent, as mentioned in section 1.3.

```
S --> S S
S --> e
S --> x
```

sentence = 'xxx'

Figure 5-2: Infinite Ambiguity

```
S --> S
S --> x
```

sentence = 'x'

Figure 5-3: Cyclic Grammar

also extremely unlikely that a natural language grammar has dense ambiguity such as that shown in figure 5-1. It is therefore safe to conclude that our algorithm is more efficient than any existing general parsing algorithms in terms of recognition time as far as practical natural language grammars are concerned.

## 5.3. Parse Forest Representation

Some of the existing general parsing algorithms leave a well-formed substring table as their output. In our opinion, these well-formed substring tables are not appropriate as a parser's final output, because it is not straightforward to simply enumerate all possible parse trees out of the tables; another search must be involved. Thus we define a *parse forest* as a representation of all possible parse trees out of which we can trivially enumerate all trees without any substantial computation.

For most natural language grammars, our shared-packed forest representation, described in section 2.4, takes less than or equal to $O(n^3)$ space. This representation, however, occasionally takes more than $O(n^3)$ space with densely ambiguous grammars. For example, it takes $O(n^5)$ space with the grammar in figure 5-1.

Earley, on the other hand, gave in his book [20] a parse forest representation which takes at most $O(n^3)$ space for arbitrary context-free grammars. However, the next section shows that his representation has a defect, and should not be used in natural language processing.[7]

---

[7]Several existing chart parsers seem to build a parse forest by adding pointers between edges. Since none of them gave a specification of the parse forest representation, we cannot make any comparisons. In any event, however, if they adopt Earley's representation then they must have the defect, and if they adopt our representation then they must occasionally take more than $O(n^3)$ time.

There exist some other algorithms that produce a parse forest in $O(n^3)$ space, but they require their grammars to be Chomsky Normal Form (CNF). Theoretically speaking every context-free grammar can be mechanically transformed into CNF. Practically speaking, however, it is usually not a good idea to mechanically transform a grammar into CNF, because the parse forest obtained from a CNF grammar will make little sense in practical applications; it is often hard to figure out a parse forest in accordance with its original grammar.

## 5.4. The Defect of Earley's Forest Representation

This section identifies the defect of Earley's representation. Consider the following grammar G1 and the sentence in figure 5-4. Figure 5-5 is the parse forest produced by Earley's algorithm. The individual trees underlying in this representation are shown in figure 5-6. They are exactly what should be produced from the grammar and the sentence.

```
S  --> e
S  --> S J
J  --> F
J  --> I
F  --> x
I  --> x
sentence = 'xx'
```

**Figure 5-4:** Grammar G1

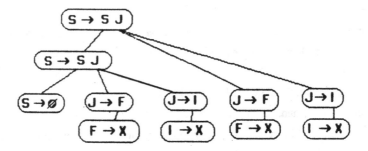

**Figure 5-5:** Earley's Parse Forest

Next consider the grammar G2 and the sentence in figure 5-7.

The two possible parse trees out of this sentence are shown in figure 5-8.

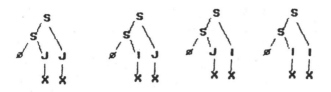

**Figure 5-6:** Underlying Parse Trees

```
S --> S S
S --> x
```

```
sentence = 'xxx'
```

**Figure 5-7:** Grammar G2

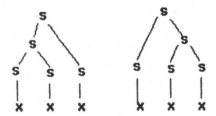

**Figure 5-8:** Correct Parse Trees

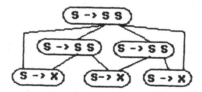

**Figure 5-9:** Defective Representation

However, Earley's parsing algorithm produces the following representation.

This representation over-represents the trees; it represents not only the intended two parse trees, but also two other incorrect trees which are shown in figure 5-10.[8]

---

[8]We could think of an algorithm that takes the defective representation as its argument, and enumerate only the intended parse trees, by checking the consistency of leaf nodes of each tree. Such an algorithm would, however, require the non-trivial amount of computation, violating our definition of parse forest.

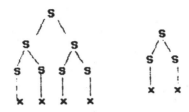

**Figure 5-10:** Wrong Parse Trees

Similarly, out of the sentence 'xxxx' with the same grammar G2, the algorithm produces a representation which over-represents 36 trees including 31 wrong trees along with 5 correct parse trees.

A grammar like G2 is totally unrealistic in the domain of programming language, and this kind of defect never appears as a real fault in that context. Productions like

    S -> SS

in G2 look rather tricky and one might suspect that such a problem would arise only in a purely theoretical argument.

Unfortunately, that kind of production is often included in practical natural language grammars. For example, one might often include a production rule like

    N -> NN

to represent compound nouns. This production rule says that two consecutive nouns can be compounded as a noun, as in 'file equipment' or 'bus driver.' This production rule is also used to represent compound nouns that consist of three or more nouns such as 'city bus driver' or 'IBM computer file equipment.' In this case, the situation is exactly the same as the situation with the grammar G2 and the sentence 'xxx' or 'xxxx', making the defect described in the previous section real in practice.

Another defective case is that using conjunctive rules such as

    NP -> NP conj NP
    VP -> VP conj VP

which are even more often included in practical grammars. The same problem as that above arises when the algorithm parses a sentence with the form:

    NP and NP and NP.....

Yet another defective case which looks slightly different but which causes the same problem is that with the following productions:

```
NP -> NP PP
PP -> prep NP
```

These represent prepositional phrase attachment to noun phrases. The fault occurs when the algorithm parses sentences with the form:

```
NP prep NP prep NP.....
```

As we have seen, it is highly likely for a practical grammar to have defective rules like those above, and we conclude that Earley's representation of a parse forest cannot be used for natural languages.

## 5.5. Summary

Our algorithm seems more efficient than any of existing the algorithms as far as practical natural language parsing is concerned, due to utilization of LR parsing tables. This claim will be supported by experiments in the next chapter. Our "shared-packed" representation of a parse forest seems to be one of the most efficient representations which do not require CNF. Our representation does not exhibit the defect found in Earley's representation.

# Chapter 6
# Empirical Results

---

## 6.1. Introduction

This chapter has two goals. The one is to show the feasibility of our algorithm in practical use. Sections 6.2 and 6.4 present this part of the discussion. The other is to support the claim that our algorithm is significantly more efficient than Earley's algorithm. Section 6.3 contains this discussion.

Before proceeding to the results, let us first describe the experiment itself. Subsection 6.1.1 describes programs used in the experiment. Similarly, subsections 6.1.2 and 6.1.3 describe grammars and sentences, respectively, which are used in the experiment. In section 6.2, the relationships between parsing time and various factors, such as sentence length, sentence ambiguity and grammar size, are observed from results of the experiment. In section 6.3, empirical comparisons between our algorithm and standard and improved version of Earley's algorithms are made. In section 6.4, several observations on space efficiency of our algorithm are made from results of the experiment. Finally, section 6.5 gives a concluding remark on the practical performance of our algorithm.

### 6.1.1. The programs

The execution time of an algorithm depends very closely on how the program is written. We can think of an almost infinite number of programming tricks that make a particular program faster. It is therefore next to impossible to measure precisely the efficiency of an algorithm or to compare precisely the efficiency of two or more algorithms by running programs. In this chapter, however, we are not trying to measure or compare efficiency of algorithms precisely. All we want to discover in this chapter is whether our algorithm is indeed efficient enough to be used in practical applications, and whether our algorithm is significantly more efficient than Earley's algorithm.

All the programs used in the experiment have been written in a manner similar to that in which most people would write from specifications. Obvious tricks are coded to make a program faster, but no odd tricks or extremely clever tricks are incorporated. For example, grammar rules are alphabetically presorted and searched using binary search, but are never encoded into internal representation for the sake of further searching efficiency. Both Earley's algorithm and our algorithm are coded in the same manner to minimize extraneous effects on the timing data.

Program I is our algorithm with an LR(0) parsing table. We have implemented in Maclisp the LR(0) table constructor as well. Program II is Earley's standard algorithm, whose specification is found in Aho and Ullman [1]. Program III is Earley's algorithm improved by Bouckaert *et al.* [8]. The improvement proceeds as follows: Whenever a new item is to be added, a function FIRST is applied to the item. The FIRST function returns a list of all possible terminals that can be the first word of the item. The item is actually added, if and only if the current word is a member of this list of terminals. This FIRST operation can be precomputed and encoded as a matrix. More details of this improvement can be found in the paper by Bouckaert *et al.* [8].

Program I, our algorithm, produces a shared-packed parse forest with all possible parses out of an ambiguous sentence, while programs II and III do not produce anything (they are recognizers). The reason why programs II and III do not produce parses is because there is no way to do so due to the defect of Earley's algorithm which was described in the previous chapter. It is expected that program I will run slightly faster if it does not produce any parses.

All programs are written in Maclisp and run on the DEC-20 in the Computer Science Department, Carnegie-Mellon University. They are not compiled, i.e., the programs are interpreted by the Maclisp interpreter. Thus, it is further expected that the programs will run several times faster, if they are compiled by a Lisp compiler. This is, however, unnecessary for our goal, because we are interested in relative parsing time, and am not particularly interested in absolute parsing time, which depends totally on the machine on which the programs run.

## 6.1.2. The sample grammars

We provide four sample grammars, grammar I, II, III and IV, for the experiment. The grammar mainly used in the experiment is grammar III, which has about 220 grammar rules. The grammar has been written only for the sake of the experiment, and is not intended for practical use. No serious consideration of linguistic issues or syntactic coverage is taken account of. The other three grammars are used to study the relationship between parsing efficiency and grammar size. Grammars I and II have 8 and 40 grammar rules, respectively, and they are nothing more than toy grammars. Grammar IV, with 400 rules, has been obtained from the Tokyo Institute of Technology [48]. The original grammar was embedded in Prolog, and a significant amount of augmentation was made by attaching arbitrary code to each rule in order to reject inappropriate parses. We, however, totally disregard all the augmentation, and use only pure context-free phrase structure of that grammar. Consequently, grammar IV becomes highly ambiguous, and could therefore be considered as one of the toughest natural language grammars in practice.

The complete list of those four sample grammars can be found in the appendix.

## 6.1.3. The sample sentences

We provide two sets of sample sentences. Sentence set I consists of 40 sentences, and most of them are taken from actual publications [57]. Only sentences which can fit grammar III with no or little modification are taken. Also, the sentences are so selected that sentence length varies fairly uniformly. The complete list of the sample sentences can be found in the appendix.

Sentence set II is made more systematically. The n-th sentence ($1 =< n =< 13$) in the set is obtained by the following schema.

noun verb det noun $(\text{prep det noun})^{n-1}$

An example sentence with this structure is:

I saw a man in the park with a telescope .....

The Ambiguity of the sentences grows as follows. This set of sentences are espcially appreciated when we study the relationship between parsing efficiency and sentence ambiguity.

| n | ambiguity |
|---|---|
| 1 | 1 |
| 2 | 2 |
| 3 | 6 |
| 4 | 14 |
| 5 | 42 |
| 6 | 132 |
| 7 | 429 |
| 8 | 1430 |
| 9 | 4862 |
| 10 | 16796 |
| 11 | 58786 |
| 12 | 208012 |
| 13 | 742900 |

Table 6-1:  Ambiguity of Sentence Set II

## 6.2. Parsing Time

The purpose of this section is to discover the relationship between the parsing time of our algorithm and the length of an input sentence, between parsing time and the ambiguity (the number of parses) of an input sentence, and between the parsing time and the size of the grammar. The parsing time is determined by CPU time minus time for garbage collection. Program I (our algorithm) is run with various grammars and input sentences described in the previous section. Programs II and III (Earley's algorithm) will be run in the next section, but not in this section.

### 6.2.1. With respect to sentence length

This subsection studies the relationship between parsing time and sentence length. We use grammar III with both sentence sets I and II. Figures 6-1 and 6-2 show that the parsing time does not grow very rapidly, as far as practical input sentences whose length is less than 35 words is concerned.

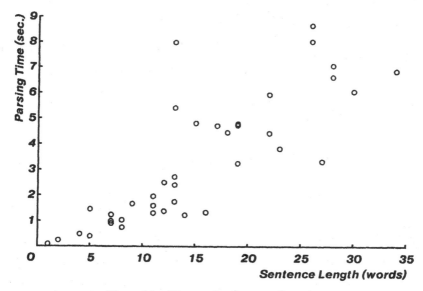

**Figure 6-1:** Time against Sentence Length
[with Grammar III and sentence set I]

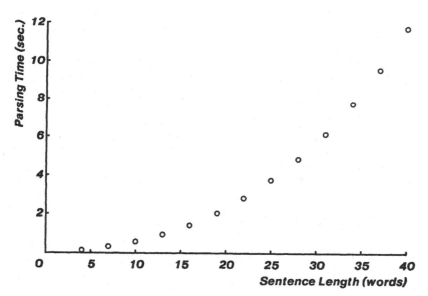

**Figure 6-2:** Time against Sentence Length
[with Grammar III and sentence set II]

### 6.2.2. With respect to sentence ambiguity

In this subsection, we present the result of the previous experiment with respect to sentence ambiguity rather than sentence length. Because the ambiguity (the number of parses) of a sentence grows exponentially as the length of the sentence grows, we use a logarithmic scale in the graphs.

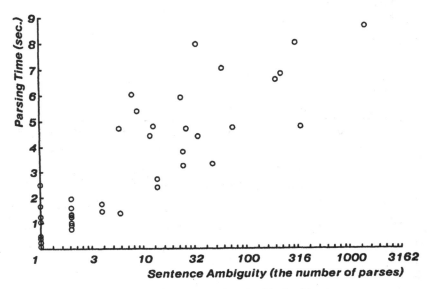

Figure 6-3: Time against Ambiguity (a)
[with Grammar III and sentence set I]

Figures 6-3 and 6-4 show, again, that the parsing time does not grow rapidly with respect to sentence ambiguity, especially considering that we have a logarithmic scale. Remember that within this parsing time, the program produces all possible parses (in a shared-packed forest).

### 6.2.3. With respect to grammar size

The same experiments as in the previous subsections are run with different grammars, to find out the relationship between parsing time and the size of grammar. The result is shown in figure 6-5. Program I parses sentence set II with grammar I, II, III and IV, and sentence set I with grammar III and IV. This subsection presents parsing times of one sentence over four different grammars. The detailed data can be found in the appendix. Because we work

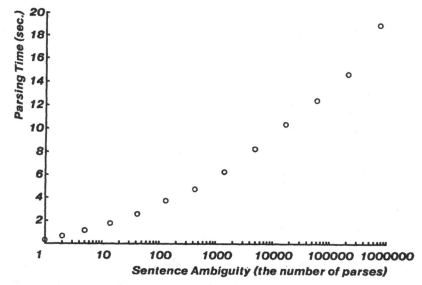

**Figure 6-4:** Time against Ambiguity (b)
[with Grammar III and sentence set II]

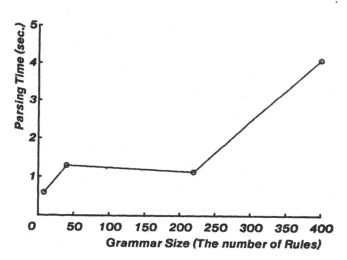

**Figure 6-5:** Time against Grammar Size
[with sentence "I saw a man in the park with a telescope."]

on only four grammars and those four grammars have been built using totally different philosophies, it is difficult to derive any strong statement out of the result presented above. However, it is safe to predict that, even with 800 rules, the parsing time should remain tractable.

## 6.3. Comparison with Earley's algorithms

This section compares our parsing algorithm with Earley's algorithm - in standard form and in an improved version - by running programs II and III with the same grammars and the same sentence sets as in the previous section.

### 6.3.1. With respect to sentence length

Figure 6-6 shows that program I, the program for our algorithm, is 5 to 10 times faster than program II, the program for Earley's standard algorithm, and still 2 to 3 times faster than program III, the program for Earley's improved algorithm. Remember that program I produces a parse forest that represents all possible parses, while program II and III do not produce anything.

The rest of this subsection and subsections 6.3.2 and 6.3.3 show the ratio between the parsing time of Earley's algorithm and that of our algorithm, under various conditions to discover in what situations our algorithm work particularly well over Earley's algorithm.

We can see from figures 6-7 and 6-8 that the Earley/Tomita ratio of parsing times is larger when the length of an input sentence is shorter.

### 6.3.2. With respect to sentence ambiguity

This subsection presents the Earley/Tomita ratio of parsing times against sentence ambiguity. We can see from figures 6-9, 6-10, 6-11 and 6-12 that the Earley/Tomita ratio is larger when an input sentence is less ambiguous.

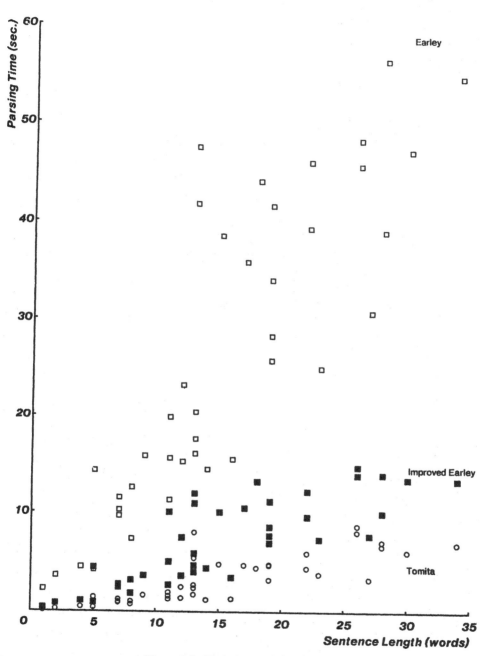

Figure 6-6:   Earley's against Tomita's
[with Grammar III and sentence set I]

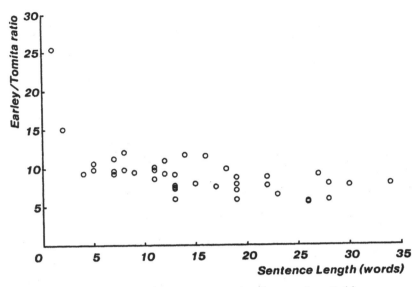

Figure 6-7: Earley/Tomita ratio against Sentence Length (a)
[Program II with Grammar III and sentence set I]

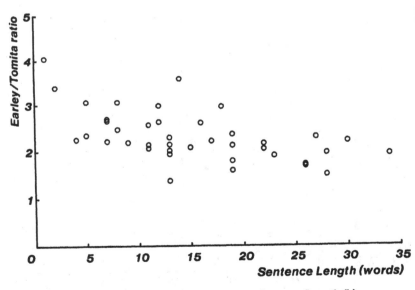

Figure 6-8: Earley/Tomita ratio against Sentence Length (b)
[Program III with Grammar III and sentence set I]

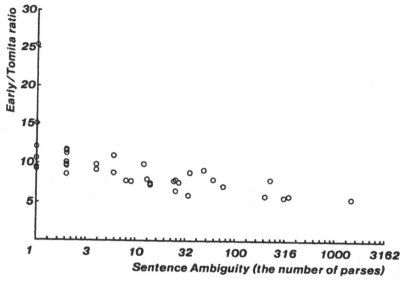

**Figure 6-9:** Earley/Tomita ratio against Sentence Ambiguity (a)
[Program II with Grammar III and sentence set I]

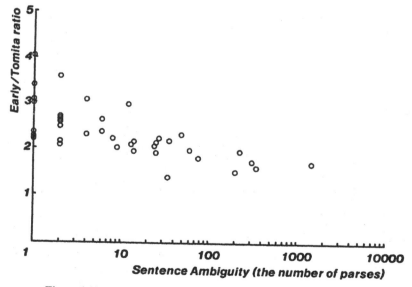

**Figure 6-10:** Earley/Tomita ratio against Sentence Ambiguity (b)
[Program III with Grammar III and sentence set I]

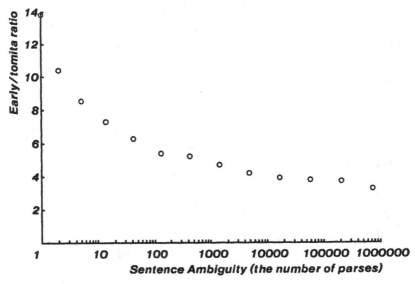

Figure 6-11:   Earley/Tomita ratio against Sentence Ambiguity (c)
[Program II with Grammar III and sentence set II]

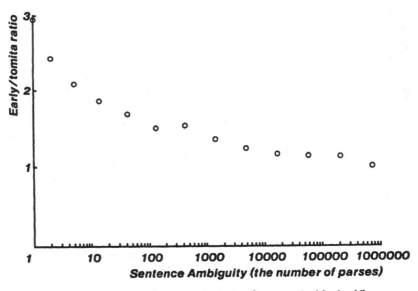

Figure 6-12:   Earley/Tomita ratio against Sentence Ambiguity (d)
[Program III with Grammar III and sentence set II]

### 6.3.3. With respect to grammar size

This subsection presents the Earley/Tomita ratio against the size of grammar. We can see from figures 6-13 and 6-14 that the Earley/Tomita ratio is larger when the size of the grammar is bigger.

The following conclusion can be made from this section 6.3.3. Our algorithm works 5 to 10 times faster than Earley's standard algorithm, and 2 to 3 times faster than Earley's improved algorithm. Earley's algorithms may perform better than our algorithm, if sentence length is extremely large, if a sentence is extremely ambiguous, or if a grammar is very small. As far as practical natural language processing is concerned, however, these conditions are unlikely to appear, and therefore it is safe to conclude that our algorithm dominates Earley's algorithms in practical natural language parsing.

## 6.4. Space Efficiency

This section discusses the space efficiency of our algorithm. Three kinds of space are used in our algorithm. The first one is for output, that is, the space needed to store a parse forest produced by program I. The second one is random access memory, or the space needed mainly to maintain the graph-structured stack. The last one is read only memory, or the space needed mainly to store parsing tables. Each kind of space efficiency is studied in turn.

### 6.4.1. Parse forest representation

Figure 6-15 shows the size of a shared-packed forest against sentence ambiguity. The variable s indicates the number of vertices in the forest. The result shows that the size of parse forest is roughly in proportion to the log of sentence ambiguity.

### 6.4.2. Graph-structured stack

Figure 6-16 shows the size of a graph-structured stack against sentence ambiguity. The variable s indicates the number of vertices in the stack. The result shows that the size of the graph-structured stack is roughly in proportion to the log of sentence ambiguity.

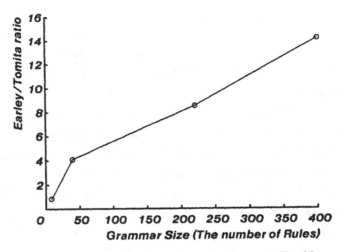

**Figure 6-13:** Earley/Tomita ratio against Grammar Size (a)
[Program II with sentence "I saw a man in the park with a telescope"]

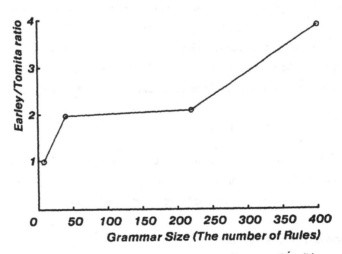

**Figure 6-14:** Earley/Tomita ratio against Grammar Size (b)
[Program III with sentence "I saw a man in the park with a telescope"]

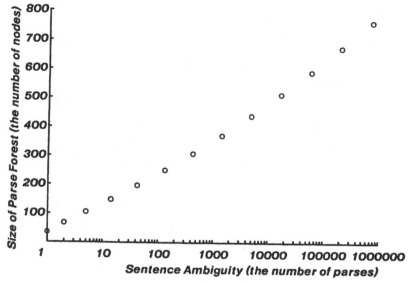

**Figure 6-15:** Size of Parse Forest against Sentence Ambiguity
[With Grammar III and sentence set II]

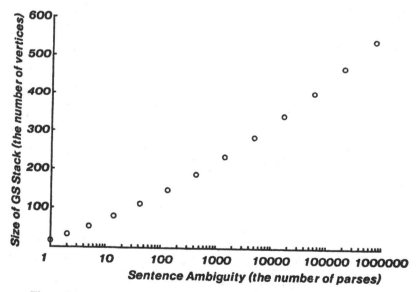

**Figure 6-16:** Size of Graph-structured Stack against Sentence Ambiguity
[With Grammar III and sentence set II]

### 6.4.3. Size of parsing tables

Theoretically speaking, the number of states (rows) in a parsing table can grow exponentially as the number of rules in its grammar grows, in the worst case. It is therefore important to make sure that the size of the parsing table remains tractable when a large grammar is used in some practical application. Figure 6-17 shows the size of the parsing table against the number of rules in the grammar. The variable s indicates the number of states in the parsing table. The result shows that the size of the parsing table is roughly in proportion to the number of rules, as far as practical natural language grammars are concerned.

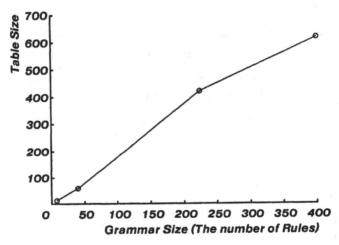

Figure 6-17:  Size of Grammar and Size of its Parsing Tables

## 6.5. Summary

It is safe to conclude in this chapter that our algorithm is significantly faster than Earley's algorithm, in the context of practical natural language processing. Also, our algorithm turns out to be feasible for use in practical applications. Its parsing time and space remain tractable when sentence length, sentence ambiguity or grammar size grows in practical applications.

The following three chapters suggest some practical applications, which make use of several advantages of our parsing algorithm, in addition to its efficiency.

# Chapter 7
# Left-to-Right On-Line Parsing

## 7.1. Introduction

One of the major characteristics of our algorithm is that an input sentence is parsed strictly from left to right. Although some other parsing algorithms, including Earley's algorithm and breath-first ATN, also have this characteristic, only a few practical systems, if any, have taken advantage of it. Taking advantage of this left-to-right-ness, we have implemented on-line parsing on the basis of our parsing algorithm. The on-line parser starts parsing as soon as the user types in the first word of a sentence, without waiting for the end of line. In this section, we describe the benefits of instantiation of on-line parsing, and discuss some of its practical applications.

## 7.2. Response Time

One obvious benefit from on-line parsing is that it reduces the parser's response time significantly. When the user finishes typing a whole sentence, most of the input sentence has been already processed by the parser. Although this does not affect CPU time, it could reduce response time from the user's point of view by about a dozen seconds or so, depending on the nature of grammar, the length of the sentence and the speed of the user's typing. On-line parsing is therefore useful in interactive systems in which input sentences are typed in by the user on line; it is not particularly useful in batch systems in which input sentences are provided in a file. An example session is presented below with the sample sentence: `I saw a man with a telescope.`

95

```
>_                                          Starts accepting a sentence.
>I_
>I _                                        Starts parsing "I".
>I s_
>I sa_
>I saw_
>I saw _                                    Starts parsing "saw".
>I saw a_
>I saw a _                                  Starts parsing "a".
>I saw a m_
>I saw a ma_
>I saw a man_
>I saw a man _                              Starts parsing "man".
>I saw a man w_
>I saw a man wi_
>I saw a man wit_
>I saw a man with_
>I saw a man with _                         Starts parsing "with".
>I saw a man with a_
>I saw a man with a _                       Starts parsing "a".
>I saw a man with a t_
>I saw a man with a te_
>I saw a man with a tel_
>I saw a man with a tele_
>I saw a man with a teles_
>I saw a man with a telesc_
>I saw a man with a telesco_
>I saw a man with a telescop_
>I saw a man with a telescope_
>I saw a man with a telescope._ Starts parsing "telescope".
>I saw a man with a telescope.   User hits <return>. Starts parsing "$".
```

**Figure 7-1:**   Example of Online Parsing

## 7.3. Undo-ability

The user often wants to hit the 'backspace' key to correct previously input words. In the case in which these words have already been processed by the parser, the parser must be able to 'un-parse' the words, without parsing the sentence from the beginning all over again. Fortunately, due to the strict left-to-right-ness, it is relatively easy for the on-line parser to un-parse a word, compared with other non-left-to-right algorithms. To implement un-parsing, the parser must store system status each time a word is parsed. In our parsing algorithm, this is done very economically because only pointers to the graph-structured stack and the parse forest need to be stored. The example session of unparsing is presented in figure 7-2.

```
>_
>I_
>I _                          Starts parsing "I".
>I s_
>I sa_
>I saa_                       Mistyping.
>I sa_                        User hits <backspace>.
>I saw_                       Keeps going.
>I saw _                      Starts parsing "saw".
>I saw a_
>I saw a _                    Starts parsing "a".
>I saw a b_
>I saw a bi_
>I saw a big_
>I saw a big _                Starts parsing "big".
>I saw a big m_
>I saw a big ma_              User changes his mind.
>I saw a big m_
>I saw a big _
>I saw a big_                 Starts unparsing "big".
>I saw a bi_
>I saw a b_
>I saw a _
>I saw a m_
>I saw a ma_
>I saw a man_
>I saw a man _                Starts parsing "man".
>I saw a man w_
>I saw a man wi_              And so on.
```

**Figure 7-2:** Example of Undoing

## 7.4. Early Error Detection

Another benefit of on-line parsing is that it can detect an error almost as soon as the error occurs, and it can warn the user immediately. When the parser finds an error, in other words, when the parser can no longer keep parsing an input sentence, it sounds a bell and ignores any more inputs until the "backspace" key is hit by the user to unparse the ungrammatical input. An example session is presented below. This relatively simple mechanism provides a partial solution to the problem of ill-formed input, which is a general problem in man-machine communication, as discussed in the following section.

```
>_
>I_
>I _            Starts parsing "I".
>I s_
>I sa_
>I saa_        Mistyping, but user not aware.
>I saaw_
>I saaw _      Starts parsing "saaw", detects error.
>I saaw _      Sounds bell, and ignores any inputs.
>I saaw_       User hits backspace.
>I saa_
>I sa_
>I saw_
>I saw _       Starts parsing "saw".
>I saw a_
>I saw a _     Starts parsing "a".
>I saw a m_
>I saw a ma_
>I saw a man_
>I saw a many_
>I saw a many _    Starts parsing "many".
>I saw a many w_   Finishes parsing "many" with error.
>I saw a many w_   Sounds bell, ignores any inputs.
>I saw a many _    User hits backspace.
>I saw a many_     Starts unparsing "many".
>I saw a man_
>I saw a man _     Starts parsing "man".
>I saw a man w_
>I saw a man wi_
>I saw a man wit_
>I saw a man with_
>I saw a man with _   Starts parsing "with" and so on.
```

**Figure 7-3:** Example of Earley Error Detection

## 7.5. On-Line Parsing and Robust Parsing

One major problem of natural language interfaces is that the user often inputs sentences which cannot be normally handled by the system. Such a problem may be caused by the user's mistake or by some deficiency of the system. The user's mistakes include misspelling, incorrect segmentation, missing constituents, spurious constituents, out of order constituents, and constraint violation. The system's insufficiency includes unknown words and unknown structures. The user will apparently get frustrated if such a sentence is simply rejected by the system, and if the user is asked to retype a correct sentence all over again. We can think of basically two approaches to cope with this problem. One approach is to tolerate such extragrammaticalities as much as possible so that the system seldom rejects input sentences. This approach is often called *robust parsing*. The other approach is to save the user from meaningless typing and retyping as much as possible. This approach can be provided by on-line parsing. These two approaches are not mutually exclusive, however. In the rest of this section, we discuss how to cope with problems of extragrammaticality by the robust parsing approach and the on-line parsing approach. The classification of extragrammaticalities follows that of Carbonell and Hayes [11].

### 7.5.1. Lexical Level Extragrammaticalities

This level of extragrammaticality is the case where a word in a sentence cannot be found in the dictionary for some reason such as user's misspellings.

In the robust parsing approach, a misspelt word is corrected by a spelling corrector and treated as a correctly spelt word. However, spelling correction in general is a very expensive operation. Furthermore, serious problems arise in the following situations.

- One misspelt word may be corrected into many different words, causing ambiguity.
- The inflexion of a word is misspelt (e.g. dictionaries --> dictionarise). The morphological analyzer must also have some kind of spelling corrector.
- Incorrect segmentation (e.g. man with --> manwith; with --> wi th).
- Any combination of the above.

To cope with these serious problems, the system must have some really complex algorithm, and nevertheless there is no guarantee that the system can correct all such errors.

In the on-line parsing approach, a misspelt word can be easily detected immediately after the user types it in. Then, the parser warns the user that he has indeed made a spelling error, and waits until the misspelt word is corrected manually by the user. The obvious disadvantage of this approach over the robust parsing approach is that the user has to correct the word manually. The amount of work is, however, minimal, compared with a system in which the user has to retype a whole sentence all over again because of a mere single misspelt word. And, best of all, this approach is much simpler than the robust parsing approach. A system does not need to correct words, and does not have to cope with the serious problems described in the previous paragraph. Therefore, the on-line parsing approach might be the alternative approach of choice, when the fancy and expensive operations such as a spelling corrector are not available; for example on personal computers.

The ideal approach is perhaps a combination of on-line parsing and robust parsing. When the user inputs a misspelt word, the system first calls a relatively simple spelling corrector. If the misspelt word can be corrected by the system, the word is removed from the display and replaced by the correct word during parsing as in the following example.

```
>I  saw  a  man_
>I  saw  a  man  _            Starts parsing "man".
>I  saw  a  man  w_
>I  saw  a  man  wi_
>I  saw  a  man  wit_
>I  saw  a  man  witt_
>I  saw  a  man  witth_
>I  saw  a  man  witth  _     Starts parsing "witth", unknown.
>I  saw  a  man  with  _      Corrects the word automatically.
>I  saw  a  man  with  a_
>I  saw  a  man  with  a  _   Starts parsing "a", and so on.
```

**Figure 7-4:** Example of Online Spelling Correction

If the spelling corrector has some trouble in correcting the word, the system informs the user of an error and asks for a manual correction just as the on-line parsing approach in the previous paragraph. Grammatical categories of a misspelt word, which would help the spelling correction significantly, can be predicted from the LR parsing table in our parsing algorithm.

### 7.5.2. Sentential Level Extragrammaticalities

This level of extragrammaticality is that where an input sentence cannot be normally parsed even though all the words in the sentence are in the dictionary. This includes missing constituents,

e.g. **I saw a man a telescope,**

spurious constituents,

e.g. **I saw <u>a woman oh no I mean</u> a man with a telescope,**

out of order constituents,

e.g. **I with a telescope saw a man,**

and any other structures which are not explicitly covered by the system's grammar, either because the user inputs an ungrammatical sentence by mistake or because the user inputs a grammatical sentence but the system's grammar is not comprehensive enough to cover the sentence. Several robust parsing techniques, most notably those used in conjunction with case frame instantiation [27], resolve these problems by using both semantic and syntactic knowledge. Although the robust parsing approach can recover from many extragrammatical sentences, more serious problems still arise in the following situations:

- Combination of the sentential extragrammaticalities mentioned above.
- Combination of sentential and lexical extragrammaticalities.
- Sentences with a totally unexpected structure.

In most of these cases, the parser has to reject such input sentences, and ask the user to retype a whole sentence all over again.

In the on-line parsing approach, the parser warns the user as soon as the parser finds that no acceptable sentence can be derived from the words the user typed in so far, and asks the user to correct the input. The obvious disadvantage of this approach again is that the user has to correct his input manually. Unlike lexical grammaticalities, the user may have to correct not only the last input word, but also several words in front of it. However, this is still much less work, compared with a system in which the user is asked to retype a whole sentence. The advantage of this approach is again its simplicity. No expensive operations are required to cope with any sentential level extragrammaticalities, no matter how difficult for the robust parsing approach to cope with them.

The ideal solution is again perhaps to combine these two approaches. The parser tries to tolerate extragrammaticalities of an input sentence as much as possible, but it warns the user as soon as it finds itself unable to recover the extragrammaticalities any longer.

### 7.5.3. Dialog Level Extragrammaticalities

There is no way in which on-line parsing can help to resolve this level of extragrammaticalities (e.g. fragmentary or elliptical input).

## 7.6. Summary

Despite its simplicity, the on-line parsing approach provides a partial solution to the problem of ill-formed inputs. It seems that on-line parsing is more effective for lower level extragrammaticalities such as mistyping due to the user's carelessness than higher level extragrammaticalities. As we have discussed in the previous section, it would be ideal to combine the on-line parsing approach and the robust parsing approach. However, on-line parsing alone can still provide a large amount of user-friendliness, compared with a system in which the user is asked to retype a whole sentence whenever the parser encounters a difficulty. In cases where robust parsing is too expensive to implement, such as on personal computers, on-line parsing should be the alternative approach of choice in order to provide user-friendliness to a system. And even if robust parsing is available, incorporation of on-line parsing might be appreciated in cases where input sentences are so problematic that the robust parser must reject them.

# Chapter 8
# Sentence Disambiguation by Asking

## 8.1. Introduction

Our parsing algorithm produces all possible parses from an ambiguous sentence. For the algorithm to be useful in practical applications, we need a mechanism to select one intended parse out of a batch of parses. In theory, it is desirable for the system to be able to disambiguate a sentence by semantics and pragmatics, and a large number of techniques using semantic information have been developed to resolve natural language ambiguity [13, 45, 7]. In practice, however, not all ambiguity problems can be solved by those techniques at the current state of the art. Moreover, some sentences are *absolutely* ambiguous, that is, even a human cannot disambiguate them, unless he knows the intent of the speaker.

This chapter describes a technique to disambiguate a sentence by asking the user[9] interactively. Section 8.2 describes a general disambiguation algorithm, called *explanation list comparison*, which can apply to any context-free parsing algorithms. This algorithm might be too general and too primitive, and an application-specific modification may be required for the algorithm to be used in practical applications. This general algorithm has been applied to an interactive machine translation system with certain modifications, and the system is described in the next chapter. Section 8.3 then describes an improved, more efficient disambiguation algorithm which can run with our parsing algorithm and shared-packed forest representation.

---

[9] We assume that the user is the person who wrote the sentence.

## 8.2. Explanation List Comparison

Suppose a system is given the sentence:

"I saw a man with a telescope"

and the system has a phrase structure grammar including the following rules <a> - <g>:

```
<a>      S --> NP VP
<b>      S --> NP VP PP
<c>      NP --> *noun
<d>      NP --> *det *noun
<e>      NP --> NP PP
<f>      PP --> *prep NP
<g>      VP --> *verb NP
```

The system would produce two parse trees from the input sentence (I. using rules <b>,<c>,<g>,<d>,<f>,<d>; II. using rules <a>,<c>,<g>,<e>,<d>,<f>,<d>). The difference is whether the preposition phrase "with a telescope" qualifies the noun phrase "a man" or the sentence "I saw a man". The following discusses how to ask the user to select his intended interpretation without showing any kind of tree structures or phrase structure grammar rules. Our desired question for that sentence is thus something like:

1) The action "I saw a man" takes place "with a telescope"
2) "a man" is "with a telescope"
NUMBER ?

The technique to implement this is called *Explanation List Comparison*(ELC) [50]. The basic idea is to attach an *Explanation Template* to each rule. For example, each of the rules <a> - <g> would have an explanation template as follows:

```
         Explanation Template

<a>      (1) is a subject of the action (2)
<b>      The action (1 2) takes place (3)
<c>      (1) is a noun
<d>      (1) is a determiner of (2)
<e>      (1) is (2)
<f>      (1) is a preposition of (2)
<g>      (2) is an object of the verb (1)
```

Whenever a rule is employed to reduce constituents, an explanation is generated from its explanation template. Numbers in an explanation template indicate n-th constituent of the right hand side of the rule. For instance, when the rule <f>

```
PP --> *prep NP
```

matches "**with a telescope**" (*prep = "**with**"; NP = "**a telescope**"), the explanation

"(with) is a preposition of (a telescope)"

is generated. Whenever the system builds a parse tree, it also builds a list of explanations which are generated from explanation templates of all rules employed. We refer to such a list as an *explanation list.* The explanation lists of the parse trees in the example above are:

**Alternative I.**

\<b\> The action (I saw a man) takes place (with a telescope)
\<c\> (I) is a noun
\<g\> (a man) is an object of the verb (saw)
\<d\> (A) is a determiner of (man)
\<f\> (with) is a preposition of (a telescope)
\<d\> (A) is a determiner of (telescope)

**Alternative II.**

\<a\> (I) is a subject of the action (saw a man with a telescope)
\<c\> (I) is a noun
\<g\> (a man with a telescope) is an object of the verb (saw)
\<e\> (a man) is (with a telescope)
\<d\> (A) is a determiner of (man)
\<f\> (with) is a preposition of (a telescope)
\<d\> (A) is a determiner of (telescope)

In order to disambiguate a sentence, the system examines only these explanation lists, but not the parse trees themselves. Loosely speaking, when a system produces more than one parse tree, explanation lists of the trees are "compared" and the "difference" is shown to the user. The user is, then, asked to select the correct alternative.

### 8.2.1. The revised version of ELC

Unfortunately, the basic idea described so far has a problem. For instance, the difference between the two explanation lists in our example is

1)
    The action (I saw a man) takes place (with a telescope),
    (a man) is an object of the verb (saw);
2)
    (I) is a subject of the action (saw a man with a telescope),
    (a man with a telescope) is an object of the verb (saw),
    (a man) is (with a telescope);

despite the fact that the essential difference is only

1) The action (I saw a man) takes place (with a telescope)
2) (a man) is (with a telescope)

Two refinement ideas, *head* and *multiple explanations*, must be introduced to solve this problem.

### 8.2.2. Head

We define *head* as a word or a minimal cluster of words which are syntactically dominant in a group and could have the same syntactic function as the whole group if they stood alone. [10] For example, the head of "very smart players in New York" is "players", and the head of "incredibly beautiful" is "beautiful", but the head of "I love cats" is "I love cats" itself. The idea is that, whenever the system shows a part of an input sentence to the user, only the head of it is shown. To implement this idea, each rule must have a *head definition* besides an explanation template, as follows.

| Rule | Head  |
|------|-------|
| <a>  | [1 2] |
| <b>  | [1 2] |
| <c>  | [1]   |
| <d>  | [1 2] |
| <e>  | [1]   |
| <f>  | [1 2] |
| <g>  | [1 2] |

For instance, the head definition of the rule <b> says that the head of the construction "**NP VP PP**" is a concatenation of the head of the first constituent (NP) and the head of the second constituent (VP). The head of "A girl with a red bag saw a green tree with a telescope" is, therefore, "a girl saw a tree", because the head of "a girl with a red bag" (NP) is "a girl" and the head of "saw a green tree" (VP) is "saw a tree".

In our example, the explanation

(I) is a subject of the action (saw a man with a telescope)

becomes

(I) is a subject of the action (saw a man),

and the explanation

---

[10] This definition is slightly different from that in linguistics

(a man with a telescope) is an object of the verb (saw)

becomes

(a man) is an object of the verb (saw),

because the head of "saw a man with a telescope" is "saw a man", and the head of "a man with a telescope" is "a man".

The difference between the two alternatives is now:
1)
    The action (I saw a man) take place (with a telescope);
2)
    (I) is a subject of the action (saw a man),
    (a man) is (with a telescope);

### 8.2.3. Multiple explanations

In the examples we have discussed above, each rule generates exactly one explanation. In general, multiple explanations (including zero) should be generated by each rule. For example, rule <b>

    S --> NP VP PP

should have two explanation templates:

    (1) is a subject of the action (2)
    The action (1 2) takes place (3),

whereas rule <a>

    S --> NP VP

should have only one explanation template:

    (1) is a subject of the action (2).

With the idea of head and multiple explanations, the system now produces the preferred question, as we shall see below.

### 8.2.4. Revised ELC

To summarize, the system has a phrase structure grammar, and each rule is followed by a head definition followed by an arbitrary number of explanation templates.

```
Rule    Head      Explanation Template

<a>     [1 2]     (1) is a subject of the action (2)
<b>     [1 2]     (1) is a subject of the action (2)
                  The action (1 2) takes place (3)
<c>     [1]       <<none>>
<d>     [1 2]     (1) is a determiner of (2)
<e>     [1]       (1) is (2)
<f>     [1 2]     (1) is a preposition of (2)
<g>     [1 2]     (2) is an object of the verb (1)
```

With the ideas of head and multiple explanation, the system builds the following two explanation lists from the sentence "I saw a man with a telescope".

**Alternative I.**

<b>    (I) is a subject of the action (saw a man)
<b>    The action (I saw a man) takes place (with a telescope)
<g>    (a man) is an object of the verb (saw)
<d>    (A) is a determiner of (man)
<f>    (with) is a preposition of (a telescope)
<d>    (A) is a determiner of (telescope)

**Alternative II.**

<a>    (I) is a subject of the action (saw a man)
<g>    (a man) is an object of the verb (saw)
<e>    (a man) is (with a telescope)
<d>    (A) is a determiner of (man)
<f>    (with is a preposition of (a telescope)
<d>    (A) is a determiner of (telescope)

The difference between these two is

The action (I saw a man) takes place (with a telescope)

and

(a man) is (with a telescope).

Thus, the system can ask the preferred question:

1) The action (I saw a man) takes place (with a telescope)
2) (a man) is (with a telescope)
Number?

### 8.2.5. More Complex Example

The example in the preceding subsections is somewhat oversimplified, in the sense that there are only two possible parses and only two explanation lists are compared. If there were three or more possible parses, comparing explanation lists is not as easy as comparing just two.

Consider the following example sentence:

I saw a man in the park with a telescope.

This sentence is ambiguous in 5 ways, and its 5 explanation lists are shown below.

**Alternative I.**

(a man) is (in the park)
(the park) is (with a telescope)
    :   :
    :   :

**Alternative II.**

(a man) is (with a telescope)
(a man) is (in the park)
    :   :
    :   :

**Alternative III.**

The action (I saw a man) takes place (with a telescope)
(a man) is (in the park)
    :   :
    :   :

**Alternative IV.**

The action (I saw a man) takes place (in the park)
(the park) is (with a telescope)
    :   :
    :   :

**Alternative V.**

The action (I saw a man) takes place (with a telescope)
The action (I saw a man) takes place (in the park)
    :   :
    :   :

with these 5 explanation lists, the system asks the user a question twice, as follows:

1) (a man) is (in the park)
2) The action (I saw a man) takes place (in the park)
NUMBER? 1

1) (the park) is (with a telescope)
2) (a man) is (with a telescope)
3) The action (I saw a man) takes place (with a telescope)
NUMBER? 3

The implementation of this is described in the following.

We refer to the set of explanation lists to be compared, $\{L_1, L_2, \ldots\}$, as $A$. If the number of explanation lists in $A$ is one; the parser will return the parse tree which is associated with that explanation list. If there is more than one explanation list in $A$, the system makes a *Qlist* (Question list). The Qlist is a list of explanations

$$\text{Qlist} = \{\, e_1, e_2, \ldots, e_n \}$$

which is shown to the user to ask a question as follows:

1) $e_1$
2) $e_2$
   .  .
   .  .
n) $e_n$
Number?

The Qlist must satisfy the following two conditions to make sure that always exactly one explanation is true.

- Each explanation list $L$ must contain at least one explanation $e$ which is also in the Qlist. Mathematically, the following predicate must be satisfied.

   $\forall L \exists e (e \in L \wedge e \in \text{Qlist})$

   This condition makes sure that at least one of the explanations in a Qlist is true.

- No explanation list $L$ in $A$ contains more than one explanation in a Qlist. That is,

   $\neg (\exists L \exists e \exists e'$
   $\quad (L \in A \wedge e \in L \wedge e' \in L \wedge e \in \text{Qlist} \wedge e' \in \text{Qlist} \wedge e \neq e'))$

   This condition makes sure that at most one of the explanations in the Qlist is true.

The detailed algorithm of how to construct a Qlist is presented in the next subsection.

Once a Qlist is created, it is presented to the user. The user is asked to select one correct explanation in the Qlist, called the *key explanation*. All explanation lists which do not contain the key explanation are removed from $A$. If $A$ still contains more than one explanation list, another Qlist for this new $A$ is created, and shown to the user. This process is repeated until $A$ contains only one explanation list.

### 8.2.6. Simple Qlist Construction Algorithm

In this subsection, we present a simple and general algorithm for Qlist construction. The algorithm, which has been implemented, usually must be modified and adapted for each application. Section 8.3 will describe a more complex algorithm for disambiguating from a shared-packed forest, which has not yet been implemented.

```
input  A : set of explanation lists
output  Qlist : set of explanations
local  e : explanation
       L : explanation list (set of explanations)
       U, C : set of explanation lists
```

1: $C \Leftarrow \phi$
2: $U \Leftarrow A$
3: Qlist $\Leftarrow \phi$
4: if $U = \phi$ then return Qlist
5: select one explanation $e$ such that
    $e$ is in some explanation list $\in U$,
    but not in any explanation list $\in C$;
    if no such $e$ exists, return ERROR
6: Qlist $\Leftarrow$ Qlist $+ \{e\}$
7: $C \Leftarrow C + \{L \mid e \in L \wedge L \in U\}$
8: $U \Leftarrow \{L \mid e \notin L \wedge L \in U\}$
9: goto 4

- The input to this procedure is a set of explanation lists, $\{L_1, L_2, \dots\}$.

- The output of this procedure is a list of explanations, $\{e_1, e_2 \dots, e_n\}$, such that each explanation list, $L_i$, contains exactly one explanation which is in the Qlist.

- An explanation list L is called *covered*, if some explanation $e$ in L is also in Qlist. L is called *uncovered*, if any of the explanations in L is not in Qlist. $C$ is a set of covered explanation lists in $A$, and $U$ is a set of uncovered explanation lists in $A$.

- 1-3: initialization. Let Qlist be empty. All explanation lists in $A$ are uncovered.

- 4: if all explanation lists are covered, quit.

- 5-6: select an explanation $e$ and put it into Qlist to cover some of uncovered not explanation lists. $e$ must be such that it does exist in any of covered explanation lists (if it does not exist, the explanation list has two explanation in $A$, violating the Qlist condition).

- 7-8: make uncovered explanation lists which are now covered by $e$ to be covered.

- 9: repeat the process until everything is covered.

## 8.3. Disambiguation out of the Shared-Packed Forest

In the previous sections, the disambiguation algorithm required all explanation lists for all possible parses. That is, even if we get a parse forest in an efficient representation, the disambiguation algorithm required the forest to be expanded into a simple enumeration of all possible independent parse trees, which is obviously undesirable. This section describes an improved disambiguation algorithm which works on the shared-packed forest without unpacking.

### 8.3.1. Focus

First, we introduce a notion of *focus*. Each explanation has a focus. To implement this, we attach a *focus definition* to each explanation template. For example, the explanation template

    `((1) is (2))`

associated with the rule

    `NP -> NP PP`

has a focus definition

    `(2).`

Thus, a focus of the explanation

    (a man) is (with a telescope),

which is generated from the explanation template, is

    (with a telescope).

This focus implies that the explanation will be presented to the user to resolve ambiguity caused by the prepositional phrase (with a telescope). We shall see the benefit of the notion of focus later in this section.

### 8.3.2. Focused Qlists

In this subsection, we describe how to generate explanations with our parsing algorithm and how to maintain the generated explanations with a shared-packed forest. Whenever the parser reduces constituents using a rule, one or more explanations are generated from explanation templates of the rule. Because the parser builds a new node (or subnode of a packed node) in the shared-packed forest whenever it does a reduce action, the generated explanations are attached to the newly created node (or subnode). Thus, the first example in chapter 3 would produce the following parse forest, if the grammar has explanation templates, focus definitions and head definitions as shown below. A focus in an explanation is underlined.

```
Rule            Head    Explanation Template                Focus

S --> NP VP     [1 2]   (1) is a subject of the action (2)   [1]
S --> S PP      [1]     The action (1) takes place (2)       [2]
NP --> *n       [1]
NP --> *det *n  [1 2]   (1) is a determiner of (2)           [1]
NP --> NP PP    [1]     (1) is (2)                           [2]
PP --> *prep NP [1 2]   (1) is a preposition of (2)          [1]
VP --> *v NP    [1 2]   (2) is an object of the verb (1)     [2]
```

**Figure 8-1:** Example Grammar and Explanation Templates with a Focus

```
 0 [*n 'I']
 1 [NP (0)]
 2 [*v 'saw']
 3 [*det 'a']
 4 [*n 'man']
 5 [NP (3 4)]     (a) is a determiner of (man)
 6 [VP (2 5)]     (a man) is an object of the verb (saw)
 7 [S (1 6)]      (I) is a subject of the action (saw a man)
 8 [*prep 'in']
 9 [*det 'the']
10 [*n 'park']
11 [NP (9 10)]    (the) is a determiner of (park)
12 [PP (8 11)]    (in) is a preposition of (the park)
13 [NP (5 12)]    (a man) is (in the park)
14 [VP (2 13)]    (a man) is an object of the verb (saw)
15 [S (1 14)      (I) is a subject of the action (saw a man)
   (7 12)]        The action (I saw a man) takes place (in the park)
16 [*prep 'with']
17 [*det 'a']
18 [*n 'scope']
19 [NP (17 18)]   (a) is a determiner of (scope)
20 [PP (16 19)]   (with) is a preposition of (a scope)
21 [NP (11 20)]   (the park) is (with a scope)
22 [NP (13 20)    (a man) is (with a scope)
   (5 23)]        (a man) is (in the park)
23 [PP (8 21)]    (in) is a preposition of (the park)
24 [VP (2 22)]    (a man) is an object of the verb (saw)
25 [S (1 24)      (I) is a subject of the action (saw a man)
   (15 20)        The action (I saw a man) takes place (with a scope)
   (7 23)]        The action (I saw a man) takes place (in the park)
```

**Figure 8-2:** Parse Forest with Explanations

Actually, we do not attach these explanations to forest nodes directly. We rather store explanations in a space outside the forest called *a set of focussed Qlists*. Each explanation has one or more pointers to forest nodes. Explanations are indexed with their focuses and classified into groups. Each group of explanations is called a *focused Qlist* or simply a *Qlist*. The set of focused Qlists generated from the example is as the following.

```
(I) is a subject of the action (saw a man)        (15 0)(7 0)(25 0)

(a man) is an object of the verb (saw)            (6 0)(14 0)(24 0)

(a) is a determiner of (man)                      (5 0)

(a) is a determiner of (scope)                    (19 0)

(the) is a determiner of (park)                   (11 0)

The action (saw) takes place (in the park)        (25 2)(15 1)
(a man) is (in the park)                          (13 0)(22 1)

The action (saw) takes place (with a scope) (25 1)
(a man) is (with a scope)                         (22 0)
(the park) is (with a scope)                      (21 0)
```

**Figure 8-3:** A Set of focused Qlists and pointers

Pointers (i, j) indicate the j-th subnode (starting from 0) of node i. Note that the explanations

(a) is a determiner of (man)

and

(a) is a determiner of (scope)

are indexed differently, because focuses of these two explanations represent different segments of the input sentence.

### 8.3.3. Shaving a Forest

Having the set of focused Qlists, we now describe how to shave the shared-packed forest by asking the user, to obtain only one tree eventually. We first define a predicate USELESS and a procedure SHAVE-NODE-OFF. A node (or subnode) is called *useless* if there is no edge to the node (i.e., if it cannot be part of a complete parse), or if one of the edges from the node has been *shaved off*. In the case of a packed node, a packed node is called *useless* if there is no edge to the node, or all of its subnodes have been shaved off. The procedure SHAVE-NODE-OFF is defined as follows.

## SHAVE-NODE-OFF(node)

- if the node is a subnode of a packed node then

    o Remove all edges from the subnode.

    o Remove the subnode from the packed node.

- else

    o Remove all edges from the node.

    o Remove all edges to the node.

    o Remove the node from the forest.

- Executing this procedure may result useless nodes. In this case, apply SHAVE-NODE-OFF recursively for all such useless nodes.

## DISAMBIGUATE(forest, set-of-focused-Qlists)

- Initialization: Shave off all useless nodes.

- Repeat Until set-of-focused-Qlists becomes empty.

    o From set-of-focused-Qlists, select one group of explanations Qlist = {$e_1$, $e_2$,...}. Note that each e in Qlist has a common focus.

    o For each e in Qlist, see if e has at least one pointer to a live node. If all pointers point to a node which was previously shaved off, then remove e from Qlist.

    o If Qlist still has two or more explanations then

        - Ask the user a question by enumerating these explanations.

        - The explanation chosen by the user is called the *key explanation*. Any other explanations in Qlist are called *wrong explanations*. We shaved off all nodes in the forest which are pointed to by the wrong explanations.

    o Remove Qlist from set-of-focused-Qlists.

The following example should make the forest shaving algorithm clear. After executing the initialization, we have a forest shown in the following figure.

Set-of-focused-Qlists initially contains groups of explanations shown in figure 8-2. All Qlists that consist of only one explanation are removed immediately from set-of-focused-Qlists, because those Qlists need not be disambiguated. We arbitrarily choose the Qlist with the common focus "in the park". We see that all pointers are pointing to a live node. Thus, the following question is asked:

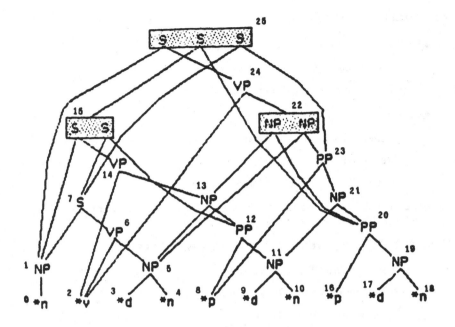

**Figure 8-4:** Forest before shaving off

1) The action (saw a man) takes place (in the park)
2) (a man) is (in the park)
Number>?

Suppose the user types "1". Then node 13 and the second subnode of node 22 are shaved off. After shaving node 13 off, we have the forest shown in figure 8-5. After shaving off the second subnode of node 22, we have the forest shown in figure 8-6. The Qlist is removed from set-of-focused-Qlists and it now consists of only a group of three explanations with the focus "with a telescope". Each explanation is checked if it points to at least one live node in the forest. The second explanation

(a man) is (with a telescope)

is then deleted because its only pointer points to node 22, which was previously shaved off. Thus, it asks the user a question showing only two explanations as follows.

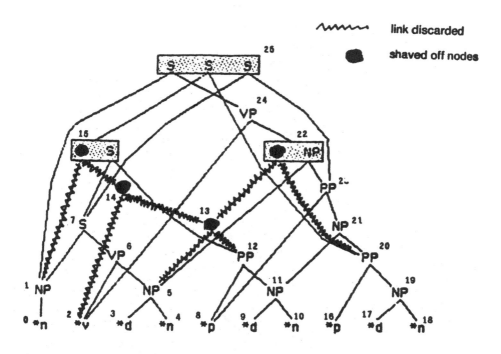

Figure 8-5: Forest after shaving off node 13

1) The action (saw a man) is (with a telescope)
2) (the park) is (with a telescope)
Number>?

Suppose the user chooses "1". Then node 21 is shaved off, and we have the forest shown in figure 8-7. This is the end of disambiguation, and we have only·one parse tree left in the shared-packed forest.

## 8.4. Summary

A frame work of how to ask questions to disambiguate sentences has been described. The idea of forest shaving described in the last section enables us to disambiguate a sentence with thousands of parses without having to deal with thousands of independent parse trees. We can now parse and disambiguate highly ambiguous sentences in an efficient manner.

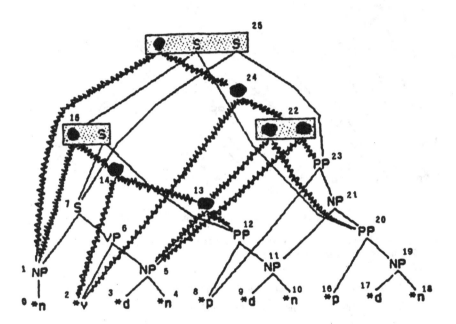

Figure 8-6:   Forest after shaving off subnode 22-1

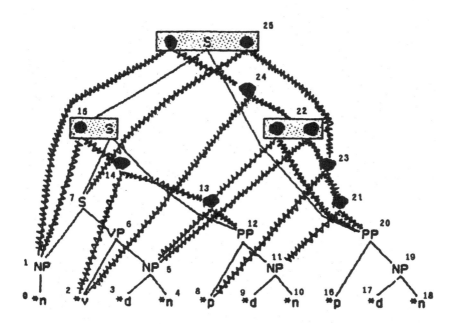

**Figure 8-7:** Final forest after disambiguation

# Chapter 9
# Interactive/Personal Machine Translation

---

## 9.1. Introduction

In this chapter, we suggest a personal machine translation system. The machine translation system described here which takes advantage of on-line parsing and interactive sentence disambiguation, has a totally different philosophy from that of conventional machine translation systems. We have implemented an experimental system by extending an existing English Japanese machine translation system,[11] to demonstrate feasibility of the interactive approach to machine translation. This pilot system adopts neither our parsing algorithm nor on-line parsing, and is far away from being practical, but some promising data have been found from experiments with the system.

## 9.2. The Design Philosophy

Most existing practical machine translation (MT) systems are designed to translate off-line large documents, such as technical papers and manuals. However, there is a growing need for translating not only large texts such as these, but also personal short texts such as letters, telexes and informal messages. The conventional MT systems, which are intended to translate large texts, are not very suitable for these kinds of small jobs, as we see later. We need a different type of system for these which, throughout this chapter, we refer to as a Machine Interpretation (MI) system, in contrast with the conventional Machine Translation (MT) systems. The MI system, however, should not be just a miniature version or extended version of the conventional MT systems. We must approach the MI systems with a totally

---

[11]This work was done with Toyoaki Nishida and Shuji Doshita at Kyoto University, Japan. The author's role in the project was to modify the parser and to implement user interaction. All part of English-Japanese machine translation system, except the user interaction, was built only by Nishida and Doshita.

different design philosophy. In the rest of this section, we contrast the design philosophy of an MI system with that of an MT system.

It seems that all practical MT systems are not fully automatic, but require human assistance in some way. The methods of human assistance can be divided into four categories:

- (1)Rejection, Sentences which the system cannot handle are rejected. Only tractable sentences are translated by the system. The rejected sentences are then translated by human translators.

- (2)Pre-editing, Source texts are edited by humans to make them fit the syntax and the vocabulary the system can handle.

- (3)Post-editing, The system takes unedited source texts and outputs target texts which require substantial human post-editing (most common method).

- (4)Interactive method, The system requires neither pre-editing nor post-editing; instead, it requires interactive human assistance during the translation.

To make an MT system practically useful, the cost of the assistance a human gives to the system must be significantly less than the cost of human translation of the entire text without a computer. This cost of human assistance is a crucial parameter in developing practically useful MT systems.

Next let us consider an MI system, that is intended to translate personal and small texts. The goal of the MI system is not primarily to reduce the cost of translating a document. Rather, the goal is to enable the user to translate a small text without a human translator or specialist, who are not available to translate one or two paragraphs immediately on demand. Because an MI system has a goal different from that of the MT systems, the conditions mentioned in the previous paragraph are not necessarily required for an MI system. In other words, the cost of human assistance is not as crucial in an MI system as the demand availability of the translator. Suppose a small text can be translated in 3 minutes by a human translator. If an MI system requires 6 minutes of non-specialist human assistance to do the job, the user probably does the job by himself using the MI system, rather than calling a human translator. It may require 30 minute overhead to find the translator, send the document, track it and so on, which must be added to the 3 minute translating time. Also, one wants results in minutes, rather than days - as typically required for translation services who queue their documents before 3 minute translation. Hence, one does not want to and may not be able to call a human translator each time one has such a small job. Thus, it is more acceptable for an MI system to count on human assistance than it is for a large scale MT system, because the MI system's jobs are always small.

On the other hand, in order to make an MI system practically workable, the system must satisfy a number of conditions that MT systems need not satisfy. First of all, in an MI system, the type of assistance required must be knowledge that all users possess, not expert knowledge requiring specialists. The system should assume that a user speaks only his own language, and does not know anything about foreign languages. Also, it should be assumed that the user is neither a computer engineer nor a linguist. Thus, the user must not be required to know the target foreign language, computer science or linguistics in general. This is because the user does not want to call any of these specialists each time he has a small job. On the contrary, an MT system can afford such specialists, as long as the total cost of human assistance is less than the cost of having human translators to do the same job without the MT system. Indeed, most existing practical MT systems require specially trained persons as post editors.

A second condition for an MI system to be practically workable is that the system response must be reasonably quick since an MI system runs on an interactive, real-time environment. The user does not want to wait for minutes to be asked each questions as he translates a small text. By contrast, since an MT system usually runs as a batch system, the response time is not such an important factor; only the time for human assistance matters.

The final condition for an MI system is that the system must be reasonably inexpensive so that every user can afford to run it in his home or office. MT systems are usually very expensive and installed only at major institutions. The user cannot bring a text to an institution each time he has a small job. Personal computers are therefore ideal for running MI systems.

To summarize, an MI system has the following tolerance. It can count on human assistance more than an MT system. However, it has 3 major constraints. It must be easy to use, respond reasonably quickly, and be affordable for every user.

## 9.3. The Design Decisions

Assuming that the user knows only his own language, we can think of two translation directions; (1) foreign language to user's language, and (2) user's language to foreign language. Direction 1 is not suitable for MI systems, because it is difficult for the user to input foreign sentences without knowledge of the foreign language. We should therefore focus on direction 2; translating sentences in the user's language into a foreign language.

It is fairly easy to show that the interactive method is the most suitable human assistance method for an MI system that translates the user's language into a foreign language. The other three methods of human assistance are inappropriate in the following ways: Rejection eventually requires a human translator for rejected sentences. To pre-edit an input text, the user must know the exact grammar and vocabulary the system can handle, and we have assumed that the user is neither a computer scientist nor linguist. Finally, to post-edit an output text, the user must know the foreign language.

In the interactive method, the user inputs a sentence. The system may then ask the user several questions, and on receiving answers, the system finally outputs a foreign sentence. The questions must be asked in the user's language, and must not require any knowledge of the foreign language, computer science or linguistics to answer them. A major concern of such an interactive system is the number of questions the system would ask the user. The toughest problem is perhaps syntactic ambiguity, which grows exponentially as sentence length grows. A sentence can easily have over a thousand possible parses. Although an MI system can count on human assistance more than MT systems, the system would not be workable if it asks, say, 30 questions per sentence. In the following sections, however, the experiment shows that syntactic ambiguity can be resolved by asking at most a couple of questions per sentence, if the system has a little semantics.

## 9.4. The Experimental Interactive System

This section describes an experimental MI system [51] which we have built at Kyoto University by extending Nishida and Doshita's English Japanese machine translation system [39], which is briefly described in the appendix. Our system asks its user questions to resolve input sentence ambiguity which cannot be resolved by the system itself. That is to say, when ambiguities are encountered, our system first tries to resolve them by the system itself using relatively simple semantics, and only ambiguities which could not be resolved by the system are resolved by asking the user interactively.

Potential users of our system are English speakers, and the system is to be used to translate English into Japanese. That is, the user inputs an English sentence, the system asks the user questions in English whenever needed, the user answers those questions and finally the system produces a (probably not fluent but) correct Japanese sentence. In doing this we make the following conditions:

- The user does not know the target language (Japanese) at all.

- The user is neither a computer specialist nor a linguist.

- Human assistance is achieved only by an interaction, and no pre- or post-editing is required.

As discussed in the previous section, this kind of system is particularly useful for translating personal and small texts.[12]    The experimental system has been implemented in Lisp on HITAC M-240H at Kyoto University. To implement sentence disambiguation by asking, we adopt the general algorithm described in chapter 8 with two modifications.

First, we divide the ambiguity into 4 categories: ambiguity by multi-part-of-speech word [Type A], ambiguity by conjunction [Type B], ambiguity by modification [Type C] and ambiguity by general and specific rules [Type D]. They are described in detail in the next section. The system resolves those four kinds of ambiguity in the order of A-B-C-D.

Second, before asking a question, the system reprints the input sentence, highlighting the focus of the question.

---

[12]Kay [33] argued that this kind of interactive machine translation systems could be practical for translating large documents as well, in the following two situations:

1. When the document is to be translated into several languages.

2. When the document is so technical that even professional translators can barely translate it.

## 9.5. Four Kinds of Ambiguities

In this section, we classify sentence ambiguity into 4 categories, as follows:

- Type A: Ambiguity by multi-part-of-speech words
- Type B: Ambiguity by conjunction
- Type C: Ambiguity by modification
- Type D: Ambiguity by general and specific pattern

To resolve each ambiguity, the system asks a question in a different manner.

### 9.5.1. Ambiguity by multi-part-of-speech words [Type A]

An example sentence with this kind of ambiguity is:

Time flies like an arrow.

Because the words, "time", "flies" and "like" are multi-part-of-speech words, several parse trees are generated. In some parse trees, the word "time" is a verb, and in other parse trees, it is a noun. The system asks questions as follows.

```
(Time) flies like an arrow
The word TIME is
1: verb
2: noun
NUMBER? 2

Time (flies) like an arrow
The word FLIES is
1: verb
2: noun
NUMBER? 1
```

The first line of each question is a copy of the input sentence, and the word being talked about is highlighted to get attention. Note that the system does not ask a question about the word "like", because the part of speech of the word can be uniquely determined after asking the two questions.

### 9.5.2. Ambiguity by Conjunction [Type B]

This kind of ambiguity occurs almost always when a sentence includes a conjunction such as "and". The example sentence is

I visited cities in Japan (and) Hawaii.

In this case, the system asks a question such as the following.

I visited cities in Japan (and) Hawaii
1: (cities) and (Hawaii)
2: (Japan) and (Hawaii)
NUMBER?

The system first reprints the input sentence, highlighting the word being talked about.

Another example is shown below.

noisy boys (and) girls
1: (noisy boys) and (girls)
2: (boys) and (girls)
NUMBER?

### 9.5.3. Ambiguity by Modification [Type C]

This includes the problem of prepositional phrase attachment as in the sentence

I saw a man with a telescope.

The question to resolve this is:

I saw a man (with a telescope)
1: (a man) is (with a telescope)
2: The action (saw a man) takes place (with a telescope)
NUMBER?

Another example with this kind of ambiguity and the question to resolve it is:

(large) file equipment
1: (file equipment) is large
2: (file) is large
NUMBER?

### 9.5.4. Ambiguity by General and Specific Rules [Type D]

Suppose that the system has specific rules such as

VP --> 'compare' + $NP_1$ + 'with' + $NP_2$

besides the general rule

VP --> VP + PP.

Then 'with $B$' in the verb phrase

compare $A$ with $B$

can modify 'compare' in two ways: "compare two objects $A$ and $B$" using the specific rule, or "compare $A$ by means of $B$" using the general rule. Since Japanese translations for these two interpretations are of course different, the system must resolve the ambiguity. The question the system asks to disambiguate the verb phrase above is

..... compare $A$ (with $B$) .....
1: (with $B$) is used idiomatically for the verb (compare)
2: (with $B$) is used not idiomatically
NUMBER?

## 9.6. Empirical Results

In this section, we describe the result of our experiment on how much interaction is required by our system to translate technical texts. We first define *the number of questions*. It is clearly not fair to count both a 2-alternative question and a 5-alternative question as 1 question. Thus, we define *the number of questions* of a n-alternative question to be n/2; that is, a 2-alternative question to be 1, a 3-alternative question to be 1.5, and so on. We think that this definition is a reasonable approximation.[13]   As a sample text to be translated by the system, we take four abstracts of papers in the area of computer science. The whole text consists of 40 sentences and 841 words, and the average length of one sentence is 21 words, not including periods. The result of the experiment with this text is as follows.

**The number of questions**
Total: 98
Per sentence: 2.45
Per word: 0.12

The result shows that, on average, the system asks roughly two to three questions per sentence. The relationship between the length of a sentence and the number of questions for the sentence is shown in the following. As we can see in the table, the longer a sentence, the more questions are needed to disambiguate it.

Our sample text, by the way, is a quotation from actual publications, and therefore was written by authors without considering the fact that the text is to be input to a machine. In contrast with this sample text, the input of our system, in general, tends to be composed by

---

[13]People, particularly information scientists, tend to think that $\log_2(n)$ is a better approximation. But this is not the case, because answering one 256-alternative question clearly requires much more effort than answering four 4-alternative questions.

| L | S | N | A |
|---|---|---|---|
| - 9 | 2 | 1.0 | 0.0 |
| 10-14 | 10 | 2.0 | 0.7 |
| 15-19 | 6 | 14.0 | 2.6 |
| 20-24 | 12 | 16.8 | 3.4 |
| 24- | 11 | 19.1 | 3.5 |

L: Length of sentence
S: The number of sample sentences
N: The number of parse trees generated per sentence
A: the number of questions per sentence

**Table 9-1:**  Sentence Length and Number of Questions

the user himself. Since the user knows that sentences he writes will be input to the system, it is expected that he does not input unnecessarily complex sentences. It is therefore interesting to do the same experiment with another sample text which is provided by a person who takes account of the fact that the text will be input to a machine.

We first gave the sample text used for the previous experiment to a native English speaker, and asked him to read and understand the text. We then asked him to rewrite the text, giving two comments as follows.

1. Your text will be input to a machine translation system, and very complex sentences may result in mis-translation.

2. Nevertheless, you do not have to feel restricted or to make special efforts.

As the result, our sample text was rewritten to 72 sentences and 878 words. The average length of a sentence in this new text is 12.2, which is almost 40% less than the original text. The result of our experiment with this new sample text is shown in the following.

**The number of questions**
Total: 64.5
Per sentence: 0.9
Per words: 0.07

As we can see, the system asks significantly fewer questions with the new sample text than with the original text in terms not only of the amount of interaction per sentence but also the total number of questions, despite the fact that both texts have the same semantic content.

Furthermore, it is detected that 28 out of the 64.5 questions are those to resolve ambiguity with the pattern "ADJ - NOUN - NOUN" such as

large file equipment

by asking a question as follows.

1) (file equipment) is large
2) (file) is large
NUMBER>?

As far as English-Japanese translation is concerned, this kind of ambiguity could be preserved in Japanese translation, and therefore it would not be meaningful to ask questions to resolve that kind of ambiguity. If we had the system pick an arbitrary alternative by itself, then the number of questions would decrease further, as shown in the following.

The number of questions
Total: 36
Per sentence: 0.5
Per word: 0.04

## 9.7. Discussions

Those data themselves are not particularly important, because the result depends heavily on the grammar of the system. We can, however, conclude at least that an interactive machine translation system does not ask the user a whole batch of questions per sentence, if the system has a little semantic knowledge.

This chapter has focused on grammatical ambiguity. Another important ambiguity is word-sense ambiguity such as is displayed in the word "pen". Our system does not ask questions to resolve the word-sense ambiguity. Since the domain from which we chose the examples has been limited to technical papers in the field of computer science, most words have only one Japanese translation, and most of the other words can be resolved by the system itself using simple semantics. However, because the semantics is not comprehensive enough, the system sometimes makes mistakes. It is therefore desirable for the system to be capable of asking questions to resolve word-sense ambiguity as well. This is particularly crucial if we think of expanding our domain.

We have further tried to reduce the number of parse trees and thus the number of questions, using simple heuristics. For example, we put to each grammatical rule a score indicating the probability of employing the rule, and we rejected all parse trees whose summation or product of scores of rules employed is not in the top 25% among others. This effort certainly reduced the number of questions, but also caused mis-translations intolerably often purely due to this simple heuristic. Considering the fact that our system's user does not know the target language (Japanese) and nobody post-edits the system's output, mis-translation is very serious. We therefore conclude that it is, in general, dangerous to attempt to reduce the number of questions by simple heuristics. However, some tasks such as letters to friends can tolerate moderate mis-translation; it would be desirable for the system to adopt to these different requirements by having a scale indicating the degree to which mis-translation can be tolerated. We call the scale "degree of toleration." With higher toleration, the system asks fewer questions and produces more mis-translations. On the other hand, with lower toleration, the system asks questions more often but produces more correct output. This is a part of future work to be completed.

Finally, we do not think that the way the experimental system asks questions is the most user-friendly one we can think of. Nevertheless, taking simplicity of the implementation into account, we think that our system is sufficiently acceptable at this stage. At least, it does not require any knowledge of the target language (Japanese) or computer science.

## 9.8. Summary

We have described the design philosophy of a personal/interactive machine translation system, and its feasibility has been studied by experiments. People tend to think that interactive sentence disambiguation is not even feasible, because the number of parses out of a highly ambiguous sentence sometimes exceeds a thousand. However, we have seen in the previous sections that the number of questions can be reduced remarkably if a system has little semantics. Furthermore, not many people have realized that, even if a sentence has a thousand different parses, it can be disambiguated by asking as few as five 4-alternative questions.

# Chapter 10
# Concluding Remarks

---

## 10.1. Summary of the Book

This book has described an efficient context-free parsing algorithm for natural languages, and has focussed on its practical value in natural language processing. The experiments have shown that this parsing algorithm seems significantly more efficient than Earley's algorithm and perhaps any other general context-free parsing algorithms, as far as practical natural language processing is concerned.

We have also introduced an efficient representation of all possible parses out of an ambiguous sentence. This representation, called a shared-packed forest, seems to be one of the most efficient representations which do not require a grammar to be Chomsky Normal Form.

Several practical applications of the algorithm have been suggested. Taking advantage of left-to-right-ness of our parsing algorithm, the notion of on-line parsing has been described and its benefits in practical systems have been discussed. An algorithm for sentence disambiguation out of the shared-packed forest by asking the user has been also described. This disambiguation algorithm, along with the parsing algorithm, enables us to parse and disambiguate a highly ambiguous sentence which has thousands of possible parses, without ever dealing with thousands of parse trees. A personal/interactive machine translation system has been introduced and its design philosophy and feasibility have been discussed.

133

## 10.2. Future Work

It might not be very hard to extend our parsing algorithm to handle cyclic grammars (and therefore general context-free grammars). A shared-packed forest produced by the extended algorithm can no longer be an acyclic graph; it must be a cyclic graph to represent infinitely many parses.

It might be also interesting to extend our algorithm to handle context-sensitive phrase structure grammars. Walters [56] gave a deterministic shift-reduce parsing algorithm for context-sensitive grammars, utilizing a parsing table similar to an LR parsing table. His algorithm works on only a small subset of context-sensitive grammars called CS(k) grammars. If a grammar is not CS(k), then its CS parsing table would have multiple entries. Our parsing algorithm might be able to apply to handle the multiple entries in the CS parsing table. If it were indeed possible, then we could write transformation-like rules, such as [NP AUX VP → AUX NP VP] to recognize interrogative sentences.

A more practical way to provide context-sensitiveness is to attach an arbitrary test and procedure to each grammar rule, just like the augmentation in the Augmented Transition Network [58].

As mentioned in chapter 10, the experimental machine translation system has been implemented merely to demonstrate the feasibility of interactive approach to machine translation. The experimental system does not adopt our efficient parsing algorithm or the shared-packed forest representation. It is the author's long term goal to build an interactive/personal machine translation system using the efficient parsing algorithm and forest representation described in this book. It is further desirable to adopt on-line parsing and the forest shaving disambiguation algorithm. The feasibility of such personal/interactive MT systems intended for practical use, possibly running on personal computers, is under investigation.

# Appendix A
# The Parsing Table Constructor

Our parsing algorithm utilizes standard LR parsing tables. Such LR parsing tables can be obtained by any existing methods. There are several variations of the LR parsing table construction algorithm; e.g. LR(0), SLR(1), LR(1), LALR(1), etc., and our parser can work with any of those. The only modification required for our parser is that each entry in the table should be a *set* of actions, rather than a single action. When conflict occurs, that is, when two or more actions are to be stored in an entry in the table, conventional table constructors either halt and report 'error', or store only one arbitrarily chosen action and give a warning. Our table constructor stores all of them as a set of actions.

In the following, we give a formal specification of the canonical LR(1) parsing table constructor. The algorithm is not due to the author, and in fact, the specification is, except for small modifications, quoted from Aho and Ullman [4].

## FIRST

If $\alpha$ is any string of grammar symbols, let FIRST($\alpha$) be the set of terminals that begin strings derived from $\alpha$. If $\alpha \Rightarrow^* e$, then e is also in FIRST($\alpha$).

To compute FIRST(X) for all grammar symbols X, apply the following rules until no more terminals or e can be added to any FIRST set.

- If X is terminal, then FIRST(X) = {X}.

- If X is nonterminal and X→a$\alpha$ is a production, then add a to FIRST(X). IF X→ e is a production, then add e to FIRST(X).

- If X→$Y_1 Y_2...Y_k$ is a production, then for all i such that all of $Y_1...Y_{i-1}$ are nonterminals and FIRST($Y_j$) contains e for j = 1, 2,..., i-1 (i.e. $Y_1 Y_2...Y_{i-1} \Rightarrow e$), add every non-e symbol in FIRST($Y_i$) to FIRST(X). If e is in FIRST($Y_j$) for all j = 1, 2,..., k, then add e to FIRST(X).

Now, we can compute FIRST for any string $X_1 X_2...X_n$ as follows. Add to FIRST($X_1 X_2...X_n$) all the non-e symbols of FIRST($X_1$). Also add the non-e symbols of FIRST($X_2$) if e is in FIRST($X_1$), the non-e symbols of FIRST($X_3$) if e is in both FIRST($X_1$)

and FIRST$(X_2)$, and so on. Finally, add e to FIRST$(X_1X_2...X_n)$ if, for all i, FIRST$(X_i)$ contains e, or $n=0$.

## LR(1) Item

An *LR(1) item* is of the form

$$[A \rightarrow \alpha.\beta \, , a],$$

where $A \rightarrow \alpha\beta$ is a production and a is a terminal or \$ called *lookahead*. Alternatively, we sometimes denote it as a 3-tuple

$$[p, j, a],$$

where p is a production $A \rightarrow \alpha\beta$ and j is an integer representing the position of the dot $(j = |\alpha|)$.

## CLOSURE

CLOSURE$(s)$ is a function that takes a set of items $s$ as its argument and returns another set of items.

CLOSURE$(s)$

- **repeat**
  - **for** each item $[A \rightarrow \alpha.B\beta \, , a]$ in $s$, each production $B \rightarrow \gamma$, and each terminal b in FIRST$(\beta a)$ such that $[B \rightarrow .\gamma \, , b]$ is not in $s$ **do** add $[B \rightarrow .\gamma \, , b]$ to $s$.
- **until** no more items can be added to $s$.
- **return** $s$.

## GOTO-ITEMS

GOTO-ITEMS$(s, X)$ is a function that takes a set of item $s$ and a grammar symbol X as its arguments, and returns another set of items.

GOTO-ITEMS$(s, X)$

- Let $s'$ be the set of items $[A \rightarrow \alpha X.\beta \, , a]$, such that $[A \rightarrow \alpha.X\beta \, , a]$ is in $s'$.
- **return** CLOSURE$(s')$.

## CONST-STATES

CONST-STATES is a procedure that constructs a set of sets of items, $C$. A special production, $S' \rightarrow S$, is introduced.

CONST-STATES

- Let $C$ be {CLOSURE({[S'→.S , $]})}.

- **repeat**

  ○ **for** each set of items $s$ in $C$ and each grammar symbol X such that GOTO-ITEMS($s$, X) is not empty and not already in $C$ **do** add GOTO-ITEMS($s$, X) to $C$.

- **until** no more sets of items can be added to $C$.

## CONST-TABLE

CONST-TABLE(G) is a procedure that takes a grammar G augmented by production S'→ S as its argument, and constructs ACTION table and GOTO-ITEMS table.

CONST-TABLE(G)

1. Construct $C=\{s_0.....s_n\}$ by CONST-STATES.

2. **for** i := 0 to n **do**

   a. If $[A→\alpha.a\beta , b]$ is in $s_i$ and GOTO-ITEMS($s_i$, a) = $s_j$, where a is terminal, then add 'shift j' to ACTION(i, a).

   b. If $[A→\alpha. , a]$ is in $s_i$, then add 'reduce p' to ACTION(i, a), where p is a production $A→\alpha$.

   c. If $[S'→S. , \$]$ is in $s_i$, then add 'accept' to ACTION(i, $).

3. **for** all state number i, and all nonterminal A **do**

   - **if** GOTO-ITEMS($s_i$, A) = $s_j$ **then** GOTO(i, A) := j

4. The initial state of the parser is the one constructed from the set containing item $[S'→.S, \$]$.

# Appendix B
# Earley's Algorithm

---

This appendix gives a specification of Earley's algorithm. The original algorithm described by Earley looks ahead k input symbols, just like the LR(k) algorithm looks ahead k input symbols. We fix k to be 1, for the sake of comparison with our algorithm, which utilizes LR(1) parsing tables.

An *Earley item* is of the form

$$\langle A \to \alpha.\beta , f, a \rangle,$$

where $A \to \alpha\beta$ is a production, f is an integer, $0 \leq f \leq n$, and a is a lookahead symbol. Alternatively, we sometimes denote it as

$$\langle p, j, f, a \rangle,$$

where p is the production $A \to \alpha\beta$, and j is an integer representing the position of the dot ($j = |\alpha|$). Note that an Earley item has one more element, f, than an LR(1) item $[A \to \alpha.\beta , a]$.

EARLEY($G, a_1 \ldots a_n$)

- add $\langle S' \to .S , 0, \$ \rangle$ to $I_0$.
- **for** i := 0 to n **do**

    o **for** each item in $I_i$ **do**

    - **if** the item is of the form $\langle A \to \alpha.B\beta , f, a \rangle$ **then do** PREDICTOR.
    - **if** the item is of the form $\langle A \to \alpha. , f, a \rangle$ **then do** COMPLETER.
    - **if** the item is of the form $\langle A \to \alpha.d\beta , f, a \rangle$ **then do** SCANNER.

    **if** $\langle S' \to S. , 0, \$ \rangle$ is in $I_n$ **then** accept **else** reject.

PREDICTOR

- **for** each production $B \to \gamma$, for some $\gamma$ **do**

    o **for** each b in FIRST($\beta$) **do** add $\langle B \to .\gamma , i, b \rangle$ to $I_i$.

COMPLETER

- **if** $a = a_{i+1}$ **then**

    o **for** each item $\langle B \rightarrow \alpha.A\beta$ , h, b$\rangle$ in $I_f$ **do** add $\langle B \rightarrow \alpha A.\beta$ , h, b$\rangle$ to $I_i$.

SCANNER

- **if** $d = a_{i+1}$ **then** add $\langle A \rightarrow \alpha d.\beta$ , f, a$\rangle$ to $I_{i+1}$.

# Appendix C
# Proof of Correctness of the Algorithm

---

## C.1. Introduction

The purpose of this appendix is to prove the correctness of our algorithm; that is, to prove that our algorithm accepts an input string $a_1...a_n$ if and only if $S \Rightarrow^* a_1...a_n$.

Section C.2 takes care of the 'only if' part; that is, the section proves that if a string $a_1...a_n$ is accepted by our algorithm, then $S \Rightarrow^* a_1...a_n$.

Section C.3, on the other hand, takes care of the 'if' part; that is, the section proves that if $S \Rightarrow^* a_1...a_n$ then our algorithm accepts the string $a_1...a_n$. It has been already proven that Earley's algorithm accepts a string $a_1...a_n$ if (and only if) $S \Rightarrow^* a_1...a_n$. Therefore, we only show that our algorithm accepts a string if Earley's algorithm accepts the string.

### Definition:

ITEMS($s$) is a function that takes a state number as its argument and returns the set of items of the state $s$.

## C.2. Soundness of the Algorithm

This section proves that if our algorithm accepts a string $a_1...a_n$, then $S \Rightarrow^* a_1...a_n$. To prove this, consider the following statements, $\Psi_1, ..., \Psi_4$.

- $\Psi_1$: Our algorithm accepts a string $a_1...a_n$.

- $\Psi_2$: There exists in $\Gamma$ a vertex $v$ such that $v \in U_n$ and ITEMS(STATE($v$)) includes the item [S'→S., \$]. (Remember that the special production, S' → S, was introduced in the previous appendices.)

- $\Psi_3$: There is a path $(v_0 \leftarrow x \leftarrow v)$ such that $v_0$ is the bottom of $\Gamma$, $(v_0 \in U_0)$, $v \in U_n$ and SYMBOL($x$)=S.

- $\Psi_4$: $S \Rightarrow^* a_1...a_n$.

141

We shall give three proofs, $\Psi_1 \Rightarrow \Psi_2$, $\Psi_2 \Rightarrow \Psi_3$, and $\Psi_3 \Rightarrow \Psi_4$. Before starting this, a number of lemmas and theorems are introduced and proven.

### Lemma 1:

GOTO(STATE($v$), b) = $s$ if and only if GOTO-ITEMS(ITEMS(STATE($v$)), b) = ITEMS($s$).

proof

Obvious from the definition of CONST-TABLE.

Q.E.D

### Lemma 2:

If ACTION(STATE($v$), b) includes 'shift $s$' then GOTO(STATE($v$), b) = $s$.

proof

By the definition of CONST-TABLE, if 'shift $s$' is in ACTION(STATE($v$), b), then GOTO-ITEMS(ITEMS(STATE($v$)), b) = ITEMS($s$). By lemma 1, GOTO(STATE($v$), b) = $s$.

Q.E.D.

### Lemma 3:

Whenever REDUCER or E-REDUCER creates a path of length 2 from a state vertex to another state vertex ($w \leftarrow x \leftarrow v$), STATE($v$)=GOTO(STATE($w$), B) holds, where B = SYMBOL($x$).

proof

Straightforward by analyzing exhaustively all cases that REDUCER or E-REDUCER creates an edge in $\Gamma$.

Q.E.D.

### Lemma 4:

Whenever SHIFTER creates a path of length 2 from a state vertex to another state vertex ($w \leftarrow x \leftarrow v$), STATE($v$)=GOTO(STATE($w$), b) holds, where b = SYMBOL($x$).

proof

Straightforward with lemma 2 by analyzing exhaustively all cases that SHIFTER creates an edge in $\Gamma$.

## Lemma 5:

Given $STATE(v) = GOTO(STATE(w), X)$, $ITEMS(STATE(v))$ includes $[A \rightarrow \alpha X.\beta, a]$ if and only if $ITEMS(STATE(w))$ includes $[A \rightarrow \alpha.X\beta, a]$.

proof

Immediate from the definition of GOTO-ITEMS and lemma 1.

Q. E. D.

## Theorem 1:

For all $v$, $x$, $w$ such that there is a path $(w \leftarrow x \leftarrow v)$, if $ITEMS(STATE(v))$ includes $[A \rightarrow \alpha X.\beta, a]$ then $ITEMS(STATE(w))$ includes $[A \rightarrow \alpha.X\beta, a]$, where $X = SYMBOL(x)$.

proof

Because a path can be created only by REDUCER, E-REDUCER or SHIFTER, by lemma 3 and 4, for all path $(w \leftarrow x \leftarrow v)$, $STATE(v) = GOTO(STATE(w), X)$, where $X = SYMBOL(x)$. By lemma 5, for all path $(w \leftarrow x \leftarrow v)$, $ITEMS(STATE(w))$ includes $[A \rightarrow \alpha.X\beta, a]$ if and only if $ITEMS(STATE(v))$ includes $[A \rightarrow \alpha X.\beta, a]$, where $X = SYMBOL(x)$.

Q. E. D.

## Theorem 2:

If $ITEMS(STATE(v))$ includes $[A \rightarrow \alpha.\beta, a]$, where $\alpha = X_1 X_2 .... X_m$, then for all path of length 2*m from $v$

$$(w \leftarrow x_1 \leftarrow u_1 \leftarrow x_2 \leftarrow u_2 \leftarrow ..... \leftarrow x_{m-1} \leftarrow u_{m-1} \leftarrow x_m \leftarrow v),$$

- SYMBOL$(x_i) = X_i$, for $1 \leq i \leq m$,
- ITEMS(STATE$(u_i)$) includes $[A \rightarrow X_1...X_i . X_{i+1}...X_m\beta, a]$, for $1 \leq i \leq m$,
- and ITEMS(STATE$(w)$) includes $[A \rightarrow .\alpha\beta, a]$.

proof

Straightforward from theorem 1 by induction.

Q. E. D.

## Corollary 1:

If ITEMS(STATE($v$)) includes [$A \rightarrow \gamma.$ , a], where $\gamma = X_1...X_m$, then for all path of length $2*m$ from $v$

$$(w \leftarrow x_1 \leftarrow u_1 \leftarrow x_2 \leftarrow u_2 \leftarrow ..... \leftarrow x_{m-1} \leftarrow u_{m-1} \leftarrow x_m \leftarrow v),$$

- SYMBOL($x_i$) = $X_i$, for $1 \le i \le m$,
- ITEMS(STATE($u_i$)) includes [$A \rightarrow X_1...X_i . X_{i+1}...X_m$, a], for $1 \le i \le m$,
- and ITEMS(STATE($w$)) includes [$A \rightarrow .\gamma$, a].

## Theorem 3:

If there is a path of length 2 in $\Gamma$ ($w \leftarrow x \leftarrow v$) such that $w \in U_h$ and $v \in U_f$, $0 \le h \le f \le n$, then

$$X \Rightarrow^* a_{h+1}...a_f$$
where $X = SYMBOL(x)$.

<u>proof</u>

Let the theorem statement be $\Psi$. We prove $\Psi$ by induction.

>*Basis*

Initially $\Gamma$ contains no path, satisfying $\Psi$ trivially.

>*Assume*

For all path so far in $\Gamma$, $\Psi$ holds.

>*Prove*

After a path ($w \leftarrow x \leftarrow v$) is newly created, $\Psi$ still holds.

>*Body of proof*

The new path can be added only by SHIFTER, REDUCER or E-REDUCER.

Case I: SHIFTER creates the path:

By analyzing exhaustively all cases that SHIFTER creates a path, it is clear that if SHIFTER creates a path ($w \leftarrow x \leftarrow v$) such that $v \in U_f$ and $w \in U_h$, then SYMBOL($x$) = $a_f$ and $h = f-1$. Substituting $X = a_f$ and $h+1 = f$, the statement

$$X \Rightarrow^* a_{h+1}...a_f$$
trivially holds, because we have

$$a_f \Rightarrow^* a_f$$

Case II: REDUCER or E-REDUCER creates the path:

Analyzing exhaustively all cases that REDUCER or E-REDUCER creates a path, it is clear that REDUCER or E-REDUCER creates a path $(w \leftarrow x \leftarrow v)$ such that $w \in U_h$ and $v \in U_f$, $0 \leq h \leq f \leq n$, if and only if there exists a vertex $v'$ such that

- $v' \in U_f$
- ITEMS(STATE($v'$)) includes $[A \rightarrow X_1 \ldots X_m \cdot, a]$, where $A = $ SYMBOL($x$),
- and there is a path of length $2*m$ from $v'$ to $w$.

By corollary 1, the path of length $2*m$

$$(w \leftarrow x_1 \leftarrow u_1 \leftarrow x_2 \leftarrow u_2 \leftarrow \ldots \leftarrow x_{m-1} \leftarrow u_{m-1} \leftarrow x_m \leftarrow v'),$$

satisfies SYMBOL($x_i$) = $X_i$, for $1 \leq i \leq m$.

Let $g(i)$ be an integer such that $u_i \in U_{g(i)}$. By induction hypothesis,

$$X_1 \overset{*}{\Rightarrow} a_{h+1} \ldots a_{g(1)}$$

$$X_2 \overset{*}{\Rightarrow} a_{g(1)+1} \ldots a_{g(2)}$$

$$\vdots \qquad \vdots$$

$$X_{m-1} \overset{*}{\Rightarrow} a_{g(m-2)+1} \ldots a_{g(m-1)}$$

$$X_m \overset{*}{\Rightarrow} a_{g(m-1)+1} \ldots a_f$$

Because there exists a production

$$A \rightarrow X_1 \ldots X_m,$$

we conclude that

$$A \overset{*}{\Rightarrow} a_{h+1} \ldots a_f$$

Q. E. D.

## Lemma 6:

If our algorithm accepts a string $a_1 \ldots a_n$, there exists in $\Gamma$ a vertex $v$ such that $v \in U_n$ and ITEMS(STATE($v$)) includes $[S' \rightarrow S. , \$]$.

proof

Our algorithm accepts a string $a_1 \ldots a_n$ if and only if ACTOR finds 'accept' action. ACTOR finds 'accept' action if and only if there exists a vertex $v$ in $U_n$ such that 'accept' $\in$ ACTION(STATE($v$), \$). Action 'accept' is in ACTION($s$, \$) if and only if $s$ includes $[S' \rightarrow S. , \$]$.

## Theorem 4:

If our algorithm accepts a string, $a_1....a_n$, then $S \Rightarrow^* a_1....a_n$.

proof

Recall the following four statements:

- $\Psi_1$: Out algorithm accepts a string $a_1...a_n$.
- $\Psi_2$: There exists in $\Gamma$ a vertex $v$ such that $v \in U_n$ and ITEMS(STATE($v$)) includes an item $[S' \rightarrow S., \$]$.
- $\Psi_3$: There is a path $(v_0 \leftarrow x \leftarrow v)$ such that $v_0$ is the bottom of $\Gamma$ ($v_0 \in U_0$), $v \in U_n$ and SYMBOL($x$)=S.
- $\Psi_4$: $S \Rightarrow^* a_1...a_n$.

$\Psi_1 \Rightarrow \Psi_2$

Immediate by lemma 6.

$\Psi_2 \Rightarrow \Psi_3$

By theorem 1, there exist two vertices $w$ and $x$ such that ITEMS(STATE($w$)) includes $[S' \rightarrow .S , \$]$, SYMBOL($x$)=S, and there is a path $(w \leftarrow x \leftarrow v)$. It is easy to show that $v_0$. the bottom of $\Gamma$, is the only vertex whose state can include $[S' \rightarrow .S , \$]$. Thus, $w= v_0$. Therefore, there is a path $(v_0 \leftarrow x \leftarrow v)$.

$\Psi_3 \Rightarrow \Psi_4$

Immediate from theorem 3, letting $w= v_0$. $h = 0$, $f = n$, and SYMBOL($x$)=S.

## C.3. Completeness of the Algorithm

This section shows that if $S \Rightarrow^* a_1...a_n$, our algorithm accepts the string $a_1...a_n$. To do so, we prove that our algorithm accepts a string if Earley's algorithm accepts the string.

Let $I_0...I_n$ be the parse lists of Earley's algorithm after parsing a string $a_1...a_n$ with grammar G. Let $\Gamma$ be the graph-structured stack after parsing the same string $a_1...a_n$ with the same grammar G.

To minimize the confusion caused by existence of two kinds of items, we denote $\langle....\rangle$ for items in Earley's algorithm and $[....]$ for items in LR algorithm and our algorithm. Note that $\langle....\rangle$ is 4-tuple while $[....]$ is 3-tuple.

## Theorem 5:

If an item $\langle p, j, f, a \rangle$ is in $I_k$, $0 \leq k \leq n$, then there exists in $\Gamma$ a vertex $v$ such that $v \in U_k$ and ITEMS(STATE($v$)) includes $[p, j, a]$.

<u>proof</u>

We show by induction that for all item $\langle p, j, f, a \rangle \in I_k$, $0 \leq k \leq n$,

- (a) There exists in $\Gamma$ a vertex $v \in U_k$ such that ITEMS(STATE($v$)) includes $[p, j, a]$.

- (b) There exists in $\Gamma$ a vertex $w \in U_f$ such that ITEMS(STATE($w$)) includes $[p, 0, a]$.

- (c) There is a path of length $2*j$ from $v$ to $w$.

>*Basis*

The first item in $I_0$ is $\langle S' \rightarrow .S, 0, \$ \rangle$.

- (a) We know that a vertex $v_0 \in U_0$ labeled $s_0$ is created in PARSE in initialization, and by definition of CONST-TABLE, ITEMS($s_0$) includes $[S' \rightarrow .S, \$]$.

- (b) Let $w = v_0$. Then $w \in U_f$ because $f = 0$, and ITEMS(STATE($w$)) includes $[S' \rightarrow .S, \$]$ as in (a).

- (c) Because $w = v_0$, there trivially exists a path of length 0 from $v_0$ to $w$.

>*Assume*

For all items in $I_0$, $I_1$, ....., $I_{k-1}$, and for all first $m-1$ th items in $I_k$, the conditions (a)(b)(c) hold.

>*Prove*

The $m$-th item in $I_k$ satisfies (a)(b)(c).

>*Body of proof*

Let $\langle p, j, f, a \rangle$ be the $m$-th item in $I_k$. The item was added by either PREDICTOR, SCANNER or COMPLETER.

- case I: If $j = 0$, the item was added by PREDICTOR.

- case II: If $j$-th symbol in the right hand side of p is terminal, the item was added by SCANNER.

- case III: If $j$-th symbol in the right hand side of p is nonterminal, the item was added by COMPLETER.

Case I:

Let the item be $\langle A \rightarrow .\gamma , f, a \rangle$.

- (a) Because $\langle A \rightarrow .\gamma , f, a \rangle$ was added by PREDICTOR, one of the first $m$-1 items in $I_k$ must be of the form $\langle B \rightarrow \alpha.A\beta , h, b \rangle$, where a is FIRST($\beta$) and f=k. By induction hypothesis on that item, there exists in $\Gamma$ a vertex $v \in U_k$ such that ITEMS(STATE($v$)) includes [B$\rightarrow \alpha.A\beta$ , b]. Then, because [A$\rightarrow .\gamma$ , a] $\in$ CLOSURE({[B$\rightarrow \alpha.A\beta$ , b]}), ITEMS(STATE($v$)) must include [A$\rightarrow .\gamma$ , a], by the definition of CONST-STATES.

- (b)(c) Trivial by letting $w = v$, because j = 0 and f = k.

Case II:

Let the item be $\langle A \rightarrow \alpha d.\beta , f, a \rangle$. Because the item is added by SCANNER, there must be an item $\langle A \rightarrow \alpha.d\beta , f, a \rangle$ in $I_{k-1}$, and $a_k = d$. By induction hypothesis on that item in $I_{k-1}$,

- (a) There exists in $\Gamma$ a vertex $u \in U_{k-1}$ such that ITEMS(STATE($u$)) includes [A$\rightarrow \alpha.d\beta$ , a].

$$-----(1)$$

- (b) There exists in $\Gamma$ a vertex $w \in U_f$ such that ITEMS(STATE($u$)) includes [A$\rightarrow .\alpha d\beta$ , a].

$$-----(2)$$

- (c) There is a path of length $2*|\alpha|$ from $u$ to $w$.

$$-----(3)$$

By (1), ACTION(STATE($u$), d) includes 'shift $s$', where ITEMS($s$) includes [A$\rightarrow \alpha d.\beta$ , a].

$$-----(4)$$

When SHIFTER does the action, it:

- creates two vertices $u'$ and $x$, labeled $s$ and d, respectively.

$$-----(5)$$

- creates two edges from $u'$ to $x$ and from $x$ to $u$.

$$-----(6)$$

- puts $w$ to $U_k$.

$$-----(7)$$

By (6), we know that there is a path of length 2 from $u'$ to $u$. By (3), there is a path of length $2*|\alpha|+2$ from $u'$ to $w$.

$$-----(8)$$

In summary, for item $\langle A \rightarrow \alpha d.\beta , f, a \rangle \in I_k$,

- (a) by (4)(5)(7), there exists in $\Gamma$ a vertex $u' \in U_k$ such that ITEMS(STATE($u'$)) includes $[A \to \alpha d.\beta, a]$.

- (b) by (2), there exists in $\Gamma$ a vertex $w \in U_f$ such that ITEMS(STATE($w$)) includes $[A \to .\alpha d\beta, a]$.

- (c) by (8), there is a path of length $2*|\alpha d| = 2*|\alpha| + 2$ from $u'$ to $w$.

Case III:

Because $\langle A \to \alpha B.\beta, f, \omega \rangle$ is added by COMPLETER, before the item is added there must be items:

- $\langle B \to \gamma., h, b \rangle \in I_k$,

- $\langle A \to \alpha.B\beta, f, a \rangle \in I_h$, and

- $\langle B \to .\gamma, h, b \rangle \in I_h$,

such that $b = \text{FIRST}(\beta)$ and $a_{k+1} = b$.

By induction hypothesis on these items, and by the fact that CLOSURE($\{[A \to \alpha.B\beta, a]\}$) includes $[B \to .\gamma, b]$, it is straightforward to show that there exist in $\Gamma$ two vertices $v \in U_k$ and $w \in U_h$ such that

- ITEMS(STATE($v$)) includes $[B \to \gamma., b]$,

$$\text{-----(1)}$$

- ITEMS(STATE($w$)) includes $[A \to \alpha.B\beta, a]$ and $[B \to .\gamma, b]$,

$$\text{-----(2)}$$

- and there is a path of length $2*|\gamma|$ from $v$ to $w$.

$$\text{-----(3)}$$

By (1), ACTION(STATE($v$), b) must include the action 'reduce p', where production p is $B \to \gamma$. When REDUCER does the action on $v$, it:

- creates in $\Gamma$ two vertices $u$ and $x$ labeled GOTO(STATE($w$), B) and B, respectively,

- creates two edges from $u$ to $x$ and from $x$ to $w$,

$$\text{-----(4)}$$

- and puts $u$ to $U_k$.

$$\text{-----(5)}$$

By (2), ITEMS(GOTO(STATE($w$), B)), i.e. ITEMS(STATE($u$)), must include $[A \to \alpha B.\beta, a]$.

$$\text{-----(6)}$$

By induction hypothesis on the item $\langle A \to \alpha.B\beta, f, a \rangle \in I_k$, there must be in $\Gamma$

- a vertex $w' \in U_f$ such that ITEMS(STATE($w'$)) includes $[\Lambda \to .\alpha B\beta, a]$,

$$-----（7）$$

- and a path of length $2*|\alpha|$ from $w$ to $w'$.

By (4), we know that there is a path of length 2 from $u$ to $w$. Thus, there is a path of length $2*|\alpha|+2$ from $u$ to $w'$.

$$-----（8）$$

In summary, for item $\langle \Lambda \to \alpha B.\beta, f, a \rangle \in I_k$,

- (a) by (6), there exists $u \in U_k$ such that ITEMS(STATE($w$)) includes $[\Lambda \to \alpha B.\beta, a]$,

- (b) by (7), there exists $w' \in U_f$ such that ITEMS(STATE($w'$)) includes $[\Lambda \to .\alpha B\beta, a]$,

- (c) and by (8), there is a path of length $2*|\alpha B| = 2*|\alpha|+2$ from $u$ to $w'$.

Q. E. D.

## Theorem 6:

if $S \Rightarrow^* a_1...a_n$, our algorithm accepts $a_1...a_n$.

proof

Earley [20] showed that if $S \Rightarrow^* a_1...a_n$ then Earley's algorithm accepts $a_1...a_n$. If Earley's algorithm accepts $a_1...a_n$ then by definition of acceptance in Earley's algorithm, there must be an item $\langle S' \to S., 0, \$ \rangle$ in $I_n$. If there is the item $\langle S' \to S., 0, \$ \rangle$ in $I_n$, then by theorem 5, there exists in $\Gamma$ a vertex $v$ such that $v \in U_n$ and ITEMS(STATE($v$)) includes $[S' \to S., \$]$. If there exists in $\Gamma$ a vertex $v$ such that $v \in U_n$ and ITEMS(STATE($v$)) includes $[S' \to S., \$]$, then, by lemma 6, our algorithm accepts the string $a_1...a_n$.

Q. E. D.

# Appendix D
# Raw Empirical Data

This appendix presents the raw emprical data obtained by the experiments. The unit of parsing time is millisecond. The following abbreviations are used.

| | |
|---|---|
| No. | Sentence number. |
| Leng | The length of the sentence (the number of words). |
| Amb | The ambiguity of the sentence (the number of parses). |
| GI | Grammar I, with 8 rules. |
| GII | Grammar II, with 40 rules. |
| GIII | Grammar III, with 220 rules. |
| GIV | Grammar IV, with 400 rules. |
| PI | Program I, Tomita's algorithm. |
| PII | Program II, Earley's algorithm. |
| PIII | Program III, Earley's improved algorithm. |
| S1 | The size of produced parse forest (the number of nodes). |
| S2 | The size of graph-structured stack (the number of vertices). |

| No. | Leng | GIII Amb | GIII PI | GIII PII | GIII PIII | GIV Amb | GIV PI | GIV PII | GIV PIII |
|-----|------|----------|---------|----------|-----------|---------|--------|---------|----------|
| 1-1 | 19 | 76 | 4751 | 33865 | 8545 | 12321 | 29265 | N/A | 70470 |
| 1-2 | 11 | 2 | 1308 | 11267 | 2707 | 11 | 7840 | | 26764 |
| 1-3 | 26 | 309 | 8023 | 45560 | 13825 | 127338 | 48658 | | 100628 |
| 1-4 | 8 | 1 | 1039 | 12555 | 3182 | | | | |
| 1-5 | 12 | 1 | 2499 | 23254 | 7448 | | | | |
| 1-6 | 13 | 4 | 1747 | 16006 | 4013 | | | | |
| 1-7 | 11 | 2 | 1959 | 19842 | 5029 | 276 | 14747 | | 47140 |
| 1-8 | 7 | 1 | 1239 | 11485 | 2745 | 9 | 3776 | | 12469 |
| 1-9 | 16 | 2 | 1334 | 15427 | 3475 | | | | |
| 1-10 | 22 | 35 | 4423 | 39178 | 9579 | 42159 | 34580 | | 99235 |
| 1-11 | 18 | 12 | 4448 | 44028 | 13173 | | | | |
| 1-12 | 19 | 6 | 4724 | 41509 | 11139 | | | | |
| 1-13 | 19 | 25 | 3255 | 25749 | 6918 | 432 | 16338 | | 49671 |
| 1-14 | 12 | 6 | 1382 | 15179 | 3632 | 24 | 8057 | | 28628 |
| 1-15 | 11 | 2 | 1592 | 15532 | 3415 | 12 | 13658 | | 48795 |
| 1-16 | 15 | 13 | 4807 | 38433 | 10032 | | | | |
| 1-17 | 13 | 9 | 5399 | 41726 | 10905 | 624 | 22247 | | 57285 |
| 1-18 | 17 | 27 | 4711 | 35728 | 10456 | | | | |
| 1-19 | 27 | 48 | 3330 | 30552 | 7666 | | | | |
| 1-20 | 13 | 14 | 2722 | 20385 | 5847 | 2 | 2578 | | 10037 |
| 1-21 | 19 | 346 | 4791 | 28180 | 7660 | 6304 | 61246 | | 115267 |
| 1-22 | 14 | 2 | 1229 | 14401 | 4406 | | | | |
| 1-23 | 13 | 14 | 2403 | 17551 | 4671 | | | | |
| 1-24 | 7 | 2 | 997 | 9630 | 2640 | 1 | 1767 | | 7925 |
| 1-25 | 7 | 2 | 911 | 10242 | 2450 | 12 | 4644 | | 15893 |
| 1-26 | 9 | 1 | 1663 | 15757 | 3643 | 5 | 2399 | | 9803 |
| 1-27 | 13 | 34 | 7975 | 47454 | 11926 | 3475 | 33378 | | 73878 |
| 1-28 | 34 | 224 | 6837 | 54446 | 13281 | | | | |
| 1-29 | 8 | 2 | 745 | 7313 | 1839 | 3 | 3207 | | 10456 |
| 1-30 | 28 | 60 | 7051 | 56194 | 13868 | | | | |
| 1-31 | 22 | 24 | 5926 | 45942 | 12166 | 22428 | 70723 | | 171718 |
| 1-32 | 30 | 8 | 6043 | 46991 | 13380 | | | | |
| 1-33 | 28 | 199 | 6608 | 38790 | 9949 | | | | |
| 1-34 | 26 | 1464 | 8664 | 48096 | 14647 | 4923 | 36245 | | 92911 |
| 1-35 | 23 | 25 | 3822 | 24950 | 7294 | 19773 | 100007 | | 192041 |
| 1-36 | 1 | 1 | 89 | 2261 | 360 | 1 | 235 | | 2596 |
| 1-37 | 2 | 1 | 240 | 3615 | 814 | 1 | 662 | | 5610 |
| 1-38 | 4 | 1 | 482 | 4499 | 1087 | 1 | 1203 | | 6676 |
| 1-39 | 5 | 1 | 396 | 4213 | 927 | 1 | 665 | | 3653 |
| 1-40 | 5 | 4 | 1449 | 14245 | 4439 | 34 | 6156 | | 30901 |

Table D-1: Parsing Time on Sentence Set I

| No. | Leng | Amb | GI PI | GI PII | GI PIII | GII PI | GII PII | GII PIII |
|-----|------|-----|-------|--------|---------|--------|---------|----------|
| 2-1 | 4 | 1 | 143 | 170 | 190 | 405 | 2511 | 1074 |
| 2-2 | 7 | 2 | 337 | 325 | 367 | 722 | 3680 | 1780 |
| 2-3 | 10 | 5 | 584 | 499 | 573 | 1297 | 5305 | 2551 |
| 2-4 | 13 | 14 | 953 | 709 | 859 | 2047 | 7290 | 3517 |
| 2-5 | 16 | 42 | 1419 | 974 | 1176 | 3172 | 9542 | 4746 |
| 2-6 | 19 | 132 | 2037 | 1296 | 1585 | 4621 | 12362 | 6059 |
| 2-7 | 22 | 429 | 2804 | 1685 | 2038 | 6404 | 15296 | 7871 |
| 2-8 | 25 | 1430 | 3754 | 2122 | 2623 | 8613 | 18325 | 9741 |
| 2-9 | 28 | 4862 | 4849 | 2679 | 4024 | 11186 | 22336 | 11758 |
| 2-10 | 31 | 16796 | 6138 | 3243 | 4013 | 14084 | 27529 | 14090 |
| 2-11 | 34 | 58786 | 7732 | 3919 | 4804 | 18459 | 30695 | 16441 |
| 2-12 | 37 | 208012 | 9546 | 4704 | 5806 | 22538 | 35419 | 19443 |
| 2-13 | 40 | 742900 | 11700 | 5524 | 6752 | 28150 | 40586 | 22424 |

Table D-2:  Parsing Time on Sentence Set II

| No. | GIII PI | GIII PII | GIII PIII | GIV PI | GIV PII | GIV PIII |
|-----|---------|----------|-----------|--------|---------|----------|
| 2-1 | 304 | 4206 | 896 | 1046 | 22863 | 6069 |
| 2-2 | 659 | 6847 | 1602 | 2247 | 39451 | 10612 |
| 2-3 | 1133 | 9666 | 2363 | 4076 | 57790 | 15865 |
| 2-4 | 1759 | 12848 | 3263 | 6574 | 79189 | 21831 |
| 2-5 | 2572 | 16167 | 4320 | 10107 | 101758 | 28629 |
| 2-6 | 3734 | 20160 | 5585 | 14530 | 126331 | 35173 |
| 2-7 | 4740 | 24772 | 7251 | 19934 | N/A | 42752 |
| 2-8 | 6268 | 29525 | 8471 | 27112 |  | 52240 |
| 2-9 | 8272 | 34786 | 10200 | 35126 |  | 61130 |
| 2-10 | 10394 | 40886 | 12062 | 45275 |  | 70741 |
| 2-11 | 12433 | 47321 | 14166 | 56973 |  | 81582 |
| 2-12 | 14663 | 54629 | 16588 | 71081 |  | 93765 |
| 2-13 | 18967 | 62019 | 19121 | 90848 |  | 104914 |

Table D-3:  Parsing Time on Sentence Set II (cont.)

| No. | GI<br>S1 | GI<br>S2 | GII<br>S1 | GII<br>S2 | GIII<br>S1 | GIII<br>S2 | GIV<br>S1 | GIV<br>S2 |
|------|------|------|------|------|------|------|------|------|
| 2-1 | 16 | 8 | 40 | 20 | 34 | 17 | 93 | 46 |
| 2-2 | 34 | 17 | 69 | 35 | 67 | 33 | 170 | 88 |
| 2-3 | 55 | 29 | 107 | 57 | 105 | 54 | 263 | 146 |
| 2-4 | 79 | 44 | 152 | 86 | 148 | 80 | 372 | 220 |
| 2-5 | 106 | 62 | 204 | 122 | 196 | 111 | 497 | 310 |
| 2-6 | 136 | 83 | 263 | 105 | 249 | 147 | 638 | 416 |
| 2-7 | 169 | 107 | 329 | 215 | 307 | 188 | 795 | 538 |
| 2-8 | 205 | 134 | 402 | 272 | 370 | 234 | 968 | 676 |
| 2-9 | 244 | 164 | 482 | 336 | 438 | 285 | 1157 | 830 |
| 2-10 | 286 | 197 | 569 | 407 | 511 | 341 | 1362 | 1000 |
| 2-11 | 331 | 233 | 663 | 485 | 589 | 402 | 1538 | 1186 |
| 2-12 | 379 | 272 | 764 | 570 | 672 | 468 | 1820 | 1388 |
| 2-13 | 430 | 314 | 872 | 662 | 760 | 539 | 2073 | 1606 |

Table D-4: Space Efficiency of Program I

# Appendix E
# Programs Used in the Experiments

---

## E.1. Tomita's Algorithm

```
;;;;;;;;;;;;;;;;;;;;;;;;;;;;;;;;;;;;;;;;;;;;;;;;;;;;;;;;;;;;;;;;;
;                                                             ;
;             Tomita's Parsing Algorithm                      ;
;                                                             ;
;        Mac Lisp version (1984), used in the experiments.    ;
;                                                             ;
;;;;;;;;;;;;;;;;;;;;;;;;;;;;;;;;;;;;;;;;;;;;;;;;;;;;;;;;;;;;;;;;;


;;;;;;;;;;;;;;;;;;;;;;;;;;;;;;;;;;;;;;;;;;;;;;;;;;;;;;;;;;;;;;;;;
;    - Utility Functions must be loaded.                       ;
;    - Grammar rules must be set as an array named RULES,      ;
;      and must be sorted alphabetically.                     ;
;    - ACTION table and GOTO table must be set as arrays       ;
;      named TABLE1 and TABLE2.                               ;
;    - To parse the sentence "Time flies like an arrow,"      ;
;      call (PARSESENTENCE '((*N *V)(*N *V)(*V *P)(*DET)(*N))). ;
;    - Its parse forest can be found in the array named FA.    ;
;;;;;;;;;;;;;;;;;;;;;;;;;;;;;;;;;;;;;;;;;;;;;;;;;;;;;;;;;;;;;;;;;


(DEFUN FINDARC (XLIST WSET)
  (COND ((NULL XLIST) NIL)
        ((EQUAL WSET (CDR (GA (CAR XLIST)))) (CAR XLIST))
        (T (FINDARC (CDR XLIST) WSET))))

(DEFUN RESPLIT (N X L)
  (PROG NIL
    (COND ((EVEN N) (PUSH (CAR (GA X)) L)))
    (COND ((ZEROP N) (RETURN (LIST (LIST (CDR (GA X)) L))))
          (T (RETURN (APPLY 'APPEND
                        (MAPCAR 'RESPLIT- (CDR (GA X)))))))))

(DEFUN RESPLIT- (V) (RESPLIT (1- N) V L))

(DEFUN ADDSUBNODE (N L) (STORE (FA N) (APPEND (FA N) (LIST L))))
```

**155**

```
(DEFUN SYMBOL (X) (CAR (GA X)))

(DEFUN STATE (V) (CAR (GA V)))

(DEFUN CREATEVERTEX (IN LABEL)
  (COND ((EQUAL IN 'G)
         (SETQ GP (1+ GP))
         (STORE (GA GP) (LIST LABEL))
         GP)
        ((EQUAL IN 'F)
         (SETQ FP (1+ FP))
         (STORE (FA FP) (LIST LABEL))
         FP)))

(DEFUN CREATEEDGE (V X) (STORE (GA V) (APPEND (GA V) (LIST X))))

(DEFUN REDUCE2 (SW)
  (PROG (S WSET U Z M Q CAT ACT)
    (SETQ S (CAR SW))
    (SETQ WSET (CDR SW))
    (SETQ U (FIND-U-IN-USET S))
    (COND (U
           (SETQ Z (FINDARC (CDR (GA U)) WSET))
           (COND (Z (ADDSUBNODE (SYMBOL Z) L))
                 (T (SETQ M (CREATEVERTEX 'F LEFTP))
                    (ADDSUBNODE M L)
                    (SETQ Z (CREATEVERTEX 'G M))
                    (CREATEEDGE U Z)
                    (STORE (GA Z) (APPEND (GA Z) WSET))
                    (COND ((NOT (MEMBER U ASET))
                           (DO ((C CATLIST (CDR C)))
                               ((NULL C) NIL)
                               (SETQ CAT (CAR C))
                               (DO ((AC (ACTION (STATE U) CAT)
                                        (CDR AC)))
                                   ((NULL AC) NIL)
                                   (SETQ ACT (CAR AC))
                                   (COND ((EQUAL 'R (CAR ACT))
                                          (SETQ Q (CADR ACT))
                                          (COND ((AND (< 0. (LENG Q))
                                                      (NOT (MEMBER (LIST U
                           Z
                           Q)
                        RSET)))
                                                 (PUSH (LIST U Z Q)
                                                       RSET))))))))))))
          (T (SETQ M (CREATEVERTEX 'F LEFTP))
             (ADDSUBNODE M L)
             (SETQ U (CREATEVERTEX 'G S))
             (SETQ Z (CREATEVERTEX 'G M))
             (CREATEEDGE U Z)
```

```lisp
          (STORE (GA Z) (APPEND (GA Z) WSET))
          (PUSH U ASET)
          (PUSH U USET)))))

(DEFUN REDUCER NIL
  (PROG (U X P LEFTP)
    (SETQ U (CAAR RSET))
    (SETQ X (CADAR RSET))
    (SETQ P (CADDAR RSET))
    (POP RSET)
    (SETQ LEFTP (LEFT P))
    (MAPCAR 'REDUCE1 (RESPLIT (- (* 2. (LENG P)) 2.) X NIL))))

(DEFUN REDUCE1 (WSET-L)
  (PROG (WSET L SW-TABLE W)
    (SETQ WSET (CAR WSET-L))
    (SETQ L (CADR WSET-L))
    (DO ((W- WSET (CDR W-)))
      ((NULL W-) NIL)
      (SETQ W (CAR W-))
      (SETQ SW-TABLE
            (PUTASSOC (LIST (GOTO (STATE W) LEFTP) W) SW-TABLE)))
    (MAPCAR 'REDUCE2 SW-TABLE)))

(DEFUN LENG (P) (LENGTH (CADDR (RULES P))))

(DEFUN GOTO (S A) (CADR (ASSOC A (TABLE2 S))))

(DEFUN LEFT (P) (CAR (RULES P)))

(DEFUN ACTION (S C)
  (OR (APPEND (CDR (ASSOC '@ALL (TABLE1 S)))
              (CDR (ASSOC C (TABLE1 S))))
      (CDR (ASSOC '*ELSE (TABLE1 S)))))

(DEFUN FIND-U-IN-USET (S)
  (DO ((USET- USET (CDR USET-)))
    ((NULL USET-) NIL)
    (COND ((EQUAL S (CAR (GA (CAR USET-)))) (RETURN (CAR USET-))))))


(DEFUN PARSEWORD (CATLIST)
  (PROG (RESET RSET QSET ASET)
        (SETQ R (- (RUNTIME) (STATUS GCTIME)))
        (SETQ ASET USET)
  LOOP  (COND (ASET (ACTOR))
              (RSET (REDUCER))
              (RESET (E-REDUCER)))
        (COND ((OR ASET RSET RESET) (GO LOOP)))
        (SHIFTER)
        (PRINTLINE (LIST (LENGTH USET)
```

```
                        (SETQ RR
                              (// (- (RUNTIME) (STATUS GCTIME) R)
                                  1000.))))
          (SETQ TOTALTIME (+ TOTALTIME RR))))

(DEFUN INITPARSE NIL
  (SETQ TOTALTIME 0.)
  (SETQ GP 0.)
  (SETQ FP 0.)
  (SETQ RESULT NIL)
  (ARRAY GA T 6000.)
  (ARRAY FA T 4000.)
  (STORE (GA 0.) '(0.))
  (SETQ USET '(0.)))


(DEFUN ACTOR NIL
  (PROG (V C X P ACT)
    (SETQ V (POP ASET))
    (DO ((C- CATLIST (CDR C-)))
      ((NULL C-) NIL)
      (SETQ C (CAR C-))
      (DO ((ACT- (ACTION (STATE V) C) (CDR ACT-)))
        ((NULL ACT-) NIL)
        (SETQ ACT (CAR ACT-))
        (COND ((EQ (CAR ACT) 'S)
                (PUSH (LIST V C (CADR ACT)) QSET))
              ((EQ (CAR ACT) 'R)
                (SETQ P (CADR ACT))
                (COND ((ZEROP (LENG P))
                        (COND ((NOT (MEMBER (LIST V P) RESET))
                              (PUSH (LIST V P) RESET))))
                      (T (DO ((X- (CDR (GA V)) (CDR X-)))
                            ((NULL X-) NIL)
                            (SETQ X (CAR X-))
                            (COND ((NOT (MEMBER (LIST V X P) RSET))
                                  (PUSH (LIST V X P) RSET)))))))
              ((EQ (CAR ACT) 'A)
                (SETQ RESULT (SYMBOL (CADR (GA V)))))))))))

(DEFUN SHIFTER NIL
  (PROG (SWSET CWZSET CMSET V C S W M Z)
    (PRINC (LENGTH QSET))
    (SETQ USET NIL)
    (DO ((QSET- QSET (CDR QSET-)))
      ((NULL QSET-) NIL)
      (SETQ V (CAAR QSET-))
      (SETQ C (CADAR QSET-))
      (SETQ S (CADDAR QSET-))
      (SETQ W (CADR (ASSOC S SWSET)))
      (COND ((NULL W)
```

```
                (SETQ W (CREATEVERTEX 'G S))
                (PUSH (LIST S W) SWSET)
                (PUSH W USET)))
        (SETQ Z (CADR (ASSOC (LIST C W) CWZSET)))
        (COND ((NULL Z)
                (SETQ M (CADR (ASSOC C CMSET)))
                (COND ((NULL M)
                        (SETQ M (CREATEVERTEX 'F C))
                        (ADDSUBNODE M T)
                        (PUSH (LIST C M) CMSET)))
                (SETQ Z (CREATEVERTEX 'G M))
                (PUSH (LIST (LIST C W) Z) CWZSET)
                (CREATEEDGE W Z)))
        (CREATEEDGE Z V))))

(DEFUN E-REDUCER NIL
  (PROG (SWSET CWZSET CMSET V C S W M Z)
    (SETQ USET NIL)
    (DO ((RESET- RESET (CDR RESET-)))
      ((NULL RESET-) NIL)
      (SETQ V (CAAR RESET-))
      (SETQ C (LEFT (CADAR RESET-)))
      (SETQ S (GOTO (STATE V) C))
      (SETQ W (CADR (ASSOC S SWSET)))
      (COND ((NULL W)
              (SETQ W (CREATEVERTEX 'G S))
              (PUSH (LIST S W) SWSET)
              (PUSH W USET)
              (PUSH W ASET)))
      (SETQ Z (CADR (ASSOC (LIST C W) CWZSET)))
      (COND ((NULL Z)
              (SETQ M (CADR (ASSOC C CMSET)))
              (COND ((NULL M)
                      (SETQ M (CREATEVERTEX 'F C))
                      (ADDSUBNODE M NIL)
                      (PUSH (LIST C M) CMSET)))
              (SETQ Z (CREATEVERTEX 'G M))
              (PUSH (LIST (LIST C W) Z) CWZSET)
              (CREATEEDGE W Z)))
      (CREATEEDGE Z V))
    (SETQ RESET NIL)))

(DEFUN PARSESENTENCE (SENTENCE)
  (INITPARSE)
  (PRINTLINE SENTENCE)
  (MAPCAR 'PARSEWORD (APPEND SENTENCE '(($))))
  (COND (RESULT (LIST TOTALTIME RESULT))
        (T NIL)))
```

## E.2. Earley's Algorithm

```
;;;;;;;;;;;;;;;;;;;;;;;;;;;;;;;;;;;;;;;;;;;;;;;;;;;;;;;;;;;;;;;;;;;;
;                                                                ;
;                 Earley's Parsing Algorithm                     ;
;                                                                ;
;         Mac Lisp version (1984), used in the experiments.      ;
;                                                                ;
;;;;;;;;;;;;;;;;;;;;;;;;;;;;;;;;;;;;;;;;;;;;;;;;;;;;;;;;;;;;;;;;;;;;


;;;;;;;;;;;;;;;;;;;;;;;;;;;;;;;;;;;;;;;;;;;;;;;;;;;;;;;;;;;;;;;;;;;;
; - Utility Functions must be loaded.                             ;
; - Provide grammar rules in the same mannar as in Tomita's      ;
;   parsing algorithm.                                           ;
; - Call PARSESENTENCE function. in the same mannar as in        ;
;   Tomita's parsing algorithm.                                  ;
; - This program does not produce any parse forest.             ;
;;;;;;;;;;;;;;;;;;;;;;;;;;;;;;;;;;;;;;;;;;;;;;;;;;;;;;;;;;;;;;;;;;;;


(DEFUN GOTOITEMS (ITEMS S) (GOTO- ITEMS S))

(DEFUN GOTO- (ITEMS S)
  (COND ((NULL ITEMS) NIL)
        ((EQ (NEXTSYMBOL (CAR ITEMS)) S)
         (CONS (LIST (CAAR ITEMS)
                     (1+ (CADAR ITEMS))
                     (CADDAR ITEMS))
               (GOTO- (CDR ITEMS) S)))
        (T (GOTO- (CDR ITEMS) S))))

(DEFUN NEXTSYMBOL (ITEM)
  (COND ((= (LENGTH (CADDR (RULES (CAR ITEM)))) (CADR ITEM)) NIL)
        (T (NTH (CADR ITEM) (CADDR (RULES (CAR ITEM)))))))

(DEFUN COMPLETER NIL
  (STORE (I J)
         (UNION (I J)
                (GOTOITEMS (I (CADDR ITEM))
                           (CAR (RULES (CAR ITEM)))))))

(DEFUN SHIFTER NIL
  (COND ((MEMBER S CATLIST)
         (STORE (I (1+ J))
                (APPEND (I (1+ J))
                        (LIST (LIST (CAR ITEM)
                                    (1+ (CADR ITEM))
```

```
                              (CADDR ITEM))))))))

(DEFUN ATTACHJ (X) (LIST X 0. J))

(DEFUN PREDICTOR NIL
  (COND ((MEMBER S DONE) NIL)
        (T (PUSH S DONE)
           (STORE (I J)
                  (APPEND (I J)
                          (MAPCAR 'ATTACHJ
                                  (BISEARCHARRAY 'RULES S)))))))

(DEFUN PARSEWORD (CATLIST)
  (SETQ R (- (RUNTIME) (STATUS GCTIME)))
  (SETQ DONE NIL)
  (DO ((K 0. (1+ K)))
    ((= K (LENGTH (I J))) NIL)
    (SETQ ITEM (NTH K (I J)))
    (SETQ S (NEXTSYMBOL ITEM))
    (COND ((NULL S) (COMPLETER))
          ((TERM S) (SHIFTER))
          (T (PREDICTOR))))
  (PRINTLINE (SETQ RR (// (- (RUNTIME) (STATUS GCTIME) R) 1000.)))
  (SETQ TOTALTIME (+ TOTALTIME RR))
  (SETQ J (1+ J)))

(DEFUN PARSESENTENCE (SENTENCE)
  (ARRAY I T 50.)
  (STORE (I 0.)
         (LIST (LIST (CAR (BISEARCHARRAY 'RULES 'START)) 0. 0.)))
  (SETQ J 0.)
  (SETQ TOTALTIME 0.)
  (MAPCAR 'PARSEWORD (APPEND SENTENCE '(($))))
  (PRINTLINE (LIST (LENGTH SENTENCE) TOTALTIME))
  (LIST (LENGTH SENTENCE) TOTALTIME))
```

## E.3. Earley's Algorithm with an Improvement

```
;;;;;;;;;;;;;;;;;;;;;;;;;;;;;;;;;;;;;;;;;;;;;;;;;;;;;;;;;;;;;;;;;
;                                                               ;
;             Earley's Parsing Algorithm                        ;
;             Improved with Reachablity Test                    ;
;                                                               ;
;        Mac Lisp version (1984), used in the experiments.      ;
;                                                               ;
;;;;;;;;;;;;;;;;;;;;;;;;;;;;;;;;;;;;;;;;;;;;;;;;;;;;;;;;;;;;;;;;;


;;;;;;;;;;;;;;;;;;;;;;;;;;;;;;;;;;;;;;;;;;;;;;;;;;;;;;;;;;;;;;;;;
; - Utility Functions must be loaded.                           ;
; - Provide grammar rules in the same mannar as in Tomita's     ;
;   parsing algorithm.                                          ;
; - Build a reachability table (FIRST-TABLE), by calling        ;
;   the function (MK-FIRSTTBL).                                 ;
; - Then call PARSESENTENCE in the same mannar as in Tomita's   ;
;   parsing algorithm.                                          ;
; - This program does not produce any parse forest.            ;
;;;;;;;;;;;;;;;;;;;;;;;;;;;;;;;;;;;;;;;;;;;;;;;;;;;;;;;;;;;;;;;;;


(DEFUN GOTOITEMS (ITEMS S) (GOTO- ITEMS S))

(DEFUN GOTO- (ITEMS S)
  (COND ((NULL ITEMS) NIL)
        ((EQ (NEXTSYMBOL (CAR ITEMS)) S)
         (CONS (LIST (CAAR ITEMS)
                     (1+ (CADAR ITEMS))
                     (CADDAR ITEMS))
               (GOTO- (CDR ITEMS) S)))
        (T (GOTO- (CDR ITEMS) S))))

(DEFUN NEXTSYMBOL (ITEM)
  (COND ((= (LENGTH (CADDR (RULES (CAR ITEM)))) (CADR ITEM)) NIL)
        (T (NTH (CADR ITEM) (CADDR (RULES (CAR ITEM)))))))

(DEFUN COMPLETER NIL
  (STORE (I J)
         (UNION (I J)
                (OKITEMSONLY (GOTOITEMS (I (CADDR ITEM))
                                        (CAR (RULES (CAR ITEM))))
                             CATLIST))))

(DEFUN SHIFTER NIL
  (COND ((MEMBER S CATLIST)
```

```
              (STORE (I (1+ J))
                   (APPEND (I (1+ J))
                           (LIST (LIST (CAR ITEM)
                                       (1+ (CADR ITEM))
                                       (CADDR ITEM))))))))))

(DEFUN ATTACHJ (X) (LIST X 0. J))

(DEFUN PREDICTOR NIL
  (COND ((MEMBER S DONE) NIL)
        (T (PUSH S DONE)
           (STORE (I J)
                (APPEND (I J)
                        (OKITEMSONLY (MAPCAR 'ATTACHJ
                                             (BISEARCHARRAY 'RULES
                    S))
                                     CATLIST))))))

(DEFUN FIRST1 (S)
  (PROG (RES)
    (COND ((MEMBER S DONE) (RETURN NIL)))
    (PUSH S DONE)
    (SETQ RES NIL)
    (RETURN (COND ((TERM S) (LIST S))
                  (T (DO ((R (BISEARCHARRAY 'RULES S) (CDR R)))
                         ((NULL R) RES)
                         (DO ((L (CADDR (RULES (CAR R))) (CDR L)))
                             ((NULL L) NIL)
                             (SETQ RES (UNION (FIRST1 (CAR L)) RES))
                             (COND ((NOT (MEMBER (CAR L) NULLABLE-TBL))
                                    (RETURN NIL)))))))))))

(DEFUN MK-NULLABLE-TBL NIL
  (PROG (RES)
        (SETQ NULLABLE-TBL NIL)
    LOOP (SETQ RES NIL)
        (DO ((R RULES (CDR R)))
          ((NULL R) NIL)
          (COND ((ALL-NULLABLE (CADDAR R))
                 (SETQ RES (UNION RES (LIST (CAAR R)))))))
        (SETQ NULLABLE-TBL (APPEND RES NULLABLE-TBL))
        (COND (RES
               (DO ((L RES (CDR L)))
                 ((NULL L) NIL)
                 (SETQ RULES (DELASSQ (CAR L) RULES)))
               (GO LOOP)))))

(DEFUN ALL-NULLABLE (X)
  (COND ((NULL X) T)
        ((MEMBER (CAR X) NULLABLE-TBL) (ALL-NULLABLE (CDR X)))
        (T NIL)))
```

```
(DEFUN MK-NONTERMLIST NIL
  (SETQ NONTERMLIST NIL)
  (DO ((R RULES (CDR R)))
    ((NULL R) NIL)
    (SETQ NONTERMLIST (UNION (LIST (CAAR R)) NONTERMLIST))))

(DEFUN MK-FIRSTTBL NIL
  (PROG (DONE RULES)
    (SETQ RULES (LISTARRAY 'RULES))
    (MK-NONTERMLIST)
    (SETQ NULLABLE-TBL NIL)
    (MK-NULLABLE-TBL)
    (SETQ FIRSTTBL NIL)
    (DO ((L NONTERMLIST (CDR L)))
      ((NULL L) NIL)
      (SETQ DONE NIL)
      (PUSH (CONS (CAR L) (FIRST1 (CAR L))) FIRSTTBL))))

(DEFUN REACHABLE (S CATLIST)
  (COND ((NULL CATLIST) NIL)
        (T (OR (MEMBER (CAR CATLIST) (ASSOC S FIRSTTBL))
               (REACHABLE S (CDR CATLIST))))))

(DEFUN PARSESENTENCE (SENTENCE)
  (ARRAY I T 50.)
  (STORE (I 0.)
         (LIST (LIST (CAR (BISEARCHARRAY 'RULES 'START)) 0. 0.)))
  (SETQ J 0.)
  (SETQ TOTALTIME 0.)
  (MAPCAR 'PARSEWORD (APPEND SENTENCE '(($))))
  (PRINTLINE (LIST (LENGTH SENTENCE) TOTALTIME))
  (LIST (LENGTH SENTENCE) TOTALTIME))

(DEFUN PARSEWORD (CATLIST)
  (SETQ R (- (RUNTIME) (STATUS GCTIME)))
  (STORE (I J) (OKITEMSONLY (I J) CATLIST))
  (SETQ DONE NIL)
  (DO ((K 0. (1+ K)))
    ((= K (LENGTH (I J))) NIL)
    (SETQ ITEM (NTH K (I J)))
    (SETQ S (NEXTSYMBOL ITEM))
    (COND ((NULL S) (COMPLETER))
          ((TERM S) (SHIFTER))
          (T (PREDICTOR))))
  (PRINTLINE (SETQ RR (// (- (RUNTIME) (STATUS GCTIME) R) 1000.)))
  (SETQ TOTALTIME (+ TOTALTIME RR))
  (SETQ J (1+ J)))

(DEFUN FIRST (X)
  (COND ((NULL X) '(NIL))
```

```
        ((TERM (CAR X)) (LIST (CAR X)))
        ((NOT (MEMBER (CAR X) NULLABLE-TBL))
         (CDR (ASSOC (CAR X) FIRSTTBL)))
        (T (UNION (CDR (ASSOC (CAR X) FIRSTTBL)) (FIRST (CDR X))))))

DEFUN OKITEM (ITEM)
 (COND ((INTERSECT (CONS NIL CATLIST)
                      (FIRST (NTHCDR (CADR ITEM)
                                          (CADDR (RULES (CAR ITEM))))))
        (LIST ITEM))))

DEFUN OKITEMSONLY (ITEMS CATLIST)
 (APPLY 'APPEND (MAPCAR 'OKITEM ITEMS)))

DEFUN INTERSECT (X Y)
 (COND ((NULL X) NIL)
       ((MEMBER (CAR X) Y) T)
       (T (INTERSECT (CDR X) Y))))
```

## E.4. LR(0) Table Construction Algorithm

```
;;;;;;;;;;;;;;;;;;;;;;;;;;;;;;;;;;;;;;;;;;;;;;;;;;;;;;;;;;;;;;;;;
;                                                               ;
;            LR(0) Parsing Table Constructor                    ;
;                                                               ;
;       Mac Lisp version (1984), used in the experiments.       ;
;                                                               ;
;;;;;;;;;;;;;;;;;;;;;;;;;;;;;;;;;;;;;;;;;;;;;;;;;;;;;;;;;;;;;;;;;


;;;;;;;;;;;;;;;;;;;;;;;;;;;;;;;;;;;;;;;;;;;;;;;;;;;;;;;;;;;;;;;;;
;  - Utility Functions must be loaded.                          ;
;  - Provide grammar rules in the same mannar as in Tomita's    ;
;    parsing algorithm.                                         ;
;  - call CONSTRUCT.                                            ;
;  - Action table and GOTO table will be written in files       ;
;    named TBL1.LSP and TBL2.LSP, respectively.                 ;
;  - To run Tomita's parsing algorithm, simply load these two   ;
;    files.                                                     ;
;;;;;;;;;;;;;;;;;;;;;;;;;;;;;;;;;;;;;;;;;;;;;;;;;;;;;;;;;;;;;;;;;


(DEFUN NEXTSYMBOL (ITEM)
  (COND ((= (LENGTH (CADDR (RULES (CAR ITEM)))) (CADR ITEM)) NIL)
        (T (NTH (CADR ITEM) (CADDR (RULES (CAR ITEM)))))))

(DEFUN PUTITEMINORDER (X L)
  (COND ((NULL L) (LIST X))
        ((ITEM> X (CAR L))
         (CONS (CAR L) (PUTITEMINORDER X (CDR L))))
        (T (CONS X L))))

(DEFUN ITEM> (ITEM1 ITEM2)
  (COND ((= (CAR ITEM1) (CAR ITEM2))
         (> (CADR ITEM1) (CADR ITEM2)))
        (T (> (CAR ITEM1) (CAR ITEM2)))))

(DEFUN CLOSURE (ITEMS)
  (SETQ DONE NIL)
  (DO ((N 0. (1+ N)))
    ((= N (LENGTH ITEMS)) ITEMS)
    (SETQ S (NEXTSYMBOL (NTH N ITEMS)))
    (COND ((AND S (NOT (TERM S)) (NOT (MEMBER S DONE)))
           (PUSH S DONE)
           (SETQ ITEMS
                 (APPEND ITEMS
```

```
                            (MAPCAR 'ATTACHO (BISEARCHARRAY 'RULES S))))))
    ))

(DEFUN GOTO- (ITEMS S)
  (COND ((NULL ITEMS) NIL)
        ((EQ (NEXTSYMBOL (CAR ITEMS)) S)
         (CONS (LIST (CAAR ITEMS) (1+ (CADAR ITEMS)))
               (GOTO- (CDR ITEMS) S)))
        (T (GOTO- (CDR ITEMS) S))))

(DEFUN CONSTRUCTSETSOFITEMS NIL
  (PROG NIL
    (TERPRI)
    (PRINTLINE '|Constructing sets of items...|)
    (SETQ SETSOFITEMS
          (LIST (LIST (LIST (CAR (BISEARCHARRAY 'RULES 'START)) 0.))))
    (DO ((N 0. (1+ N)))
      ((= N (LENGTH SETSOFITEMS)) NIL)
      (PRINC (LIST N))
      (SETQ GOTOS NIL)
      (SETQ T1 NIL)
      (SETQ T2 NIL)
      (SETQ CLOSUREDITEMS (CLOSURE (NTH N SETSOFITEMS)))
      (DO ((ITEMS- CLOSUREDITEMS (CDR ITEMS-)))
        ((NULL ITEMS-) NIL)
        (SETQ S (NEXTSYMBOL (CAR ITEMS-)))
        (COND ((NULL S)
               (COND ((EQ 'START (CAR (RULES (CAAR ITEMS-))))
                      (SETQ T1 (PUTASSOC '($ (A)) T1)))
                     (T (SETQ T1
                              (PUTASSOC (LIST '@ALL
                                             (LIST 'R
                                                   (CAAR ITEMS-))
                                        T1)))))
              (T (SETQ GOTOS
                       (PUTASSOC (LIST S
                                       (LIST (CAAR ITEMS-)
                                             (1+ (CADAR ITEMS-))))
                                 GOTOS)))))
      (DO ((GOTOS- GOTOS (CDR GOTOS-)))
        ((NULL GOTOS-) NIL)
        (SETQ NEWITEMS (CDAR GOTOS-))
        (SETQ NEWITEMS (SORT NEWITEMS 'ITEM>))
        (SETQ M
              (- (LENGTH SETSOFITEMS)
                 (LENGTH (MEMBER NEWITEMS SETSOFITEMS))))
        (COND ((= M (LENGTH SETSOFITEMS))
               (SETQ SETSOFITEMS
                     (APPEND SETSOFITEMS (LIST NEWITEMS)))))
        (SETQ S (CAAR GOTOS-))
        (COND ((TERM S)
```

```
                (SETQ T1 (PUTASSOC (LIST S (LIST 'S M)) T1)))
                (T (SETQ T2 (PUTASSOC (LIST S M) T2)))))
        (PRINC T1 F1)
        (TERPRI F1)
        (PRINC T2 F2)
        (TERPRI F2))))

(DEFUN ATTACH0 (X) (LIST X 0.))

(DEFUN GOTOITEMS (ITEMS S) (GOTO- ITEMS S))

(DEFUN CONSTRUCT NIL
   (SETQ F1 (OPEN '|tbl1.lsp| '(OUT)))
   (SETQ F2 (OPEN '|tbl2.lsp| '(OUT)))
   (PRINC '|(fillarray 'table1 '(| F1)
   (TERPRI F1)
   (PRINC '|(fillarray 'table2 '(| F2)
   (TERPRI F2)
   (CONSTRUCTSETSOFITEMS)
   (PRINC '|))| F1)
   (TERPRI F1)
   (PRINC '|))| F2)
   (TERPRI F2)
   (CLOSE F1)
   (CLOSE F2))
```

## E.5. Utility Functions

```
;;;;;;;;;;;;;;;;;;;;;;;;;;;;;;;;;;;;;;;;;;;;;;;;;;;;;;;;;;;;;;;;;
;                                                             ;
;                     Utility  Functions                      ;
;                                                             ;
;                 This file must be loaded to execute         ;
;                 any programs in this appendix.              ;
;                                                             ;
;;;;;;;;;;;;;;;;;;;;;;;;;;;;;;;;;;;;;;;;;;;;;;;;;;;;;;;;;;;;;;;;;


(DEFUN UNION (L1 L2)
  (COND ((NULL L2) L1)
        ((MEMBER (CAR L2) L1) (UNION L1 (CDR L2)))
        (T (UNION (APPEND L1 (LIST (CAR L2))) (CDR L2)))))

(DEFUN TERM (X) (EQ '* (CAR (EXPLODE X))))

(DEFUN PRINTLINE (X) (PRINC X) (TERPRI))

(DEFUN BISEARCHARRAY (A KEY)
  (BISEARCHARRAY- A KEY 0. (1- (ARRAY-DIMENSION-N 1. A))))

(DEFUN BISEARCHARRAY- (A KEY ST END)
  (PROG (MID MIDKEY)
    (COND ((OR (= ST END) (> ST END))
           (COND ((SAMEPNAMEP KEY (CAR (FUNCALL A ST)))
                  (RETURN (LIST ST)))
                 (T (RETURN NIL)))))
    (SETQ MID (+ ST (// (- END ST) 2.)))
    (SETQ MIDKEY (CAR (FUNCALL A MID)))
    (COND ((SAMEPNAMEP MIDKEY KEY)
           (DO ((I (1- MID) (1- I)))
               ((OR (< I 0.) (ALPHALESSP (CAR (FUNCALL A I)) KEY))
                (SETQ ST (1+ I))))
           (DO ((I (1+ MID) (1+ I)))
               ((OR (= I (ARRAY-DIMENSION-N 1. A))
                    (ALPHALESSP KEY (CAR (FUNCALL A I))))
                (SETQ END (1- I))))
           (RETURN (LISTNM ST END))))
    (COND ((ALPHALESSP MIDKEY KEY)
           (RETURN (BISEARCHARRAY- A KEY (1+ MID) END)))
          (T (RETURN (BISEARCHARRAY- A KEY ST (1- MID)))))))

(DEFUN LISTNM (ST END)
  (DO ((L NIL (APPEND L (LIST I))) (I ST (1+ I))) ((> I END) L)))
```

```
(DEFUN PUTASSOC (X L)
  (COND ((NULL L) (LIST X))
        ((EQUAL (CAAR L) (CAR X))
         (CONS (APPEND (CAR L) (CDR X)) (CDR L)))
        (T (CONS (CAR L) (PUTASSOC X (CDR L))))))

(DEFUN REMOVEDUPL (X Y)
  (COND ((NULL X) NIL)
        ((MEMBER (CAR X) Y) (REMOVEDUPL (CDR X) Y))
        (T (CONS (CAR X) (REMOVEDUPL (CDR X) Y)))))

(DEFUN EVEN (N) (ZEROP (REMAINDER N 2.)))
```

# Appendix F
# Grammars Used in the Experiments

Four grammars, used in the experiments, are presented. A description of these grammars can be found in subsection 6.1.2.

## Grammar I

```
((NP -> (*DET *N))
 (NP -> (*N))
 (NP -> (NP PP))
 (PP -> (*PREP NP))
 (S -> (NP VP))
 (START -> (S))
 (VP -> (*V NP))
 (VP -> (VP PP))))
```

## Grammar II

```
((adjm -> (*adj))
 (adjm -> (*adj adjm))
 (adjm -> (advm *adj))
 (adjm -> (adjm *conj adjm))
 (advm -> (*adv advm))
 (advm -> (*adv))
 (advm -> (advm *conj advm))
 (dir -> (dir *conj dir))
 (dir -> (pp vp))
 (dir -> (vp))
 (dir -> (vp pp))
 (nm -> (*n))
 (nm -> (*n nm))
 (np -> (np *conj np))
 (np -> (np1 *that s))
 (np -> (np1 s))
 (np -> (np1))
 (np0 -> (nm))
 (np0 -> (adjm nm))
 (np0 -> (*det nm))
```

```
(np0 -> (*det adjm nm))
(np1 -> (adjm np0 pp pp))
(np1 -> (adjm np0 pp))
(np1 -> (adjm np0))
(np1 -> (np0 pp))
(np1 -> (np0))
(np1 -> (np0 pp pp))
(pp -> (pp *conj pp))
(pp -> (*prep np))
(s -> (np vp pp pp))
(s -> (np vp pp))
(s -> (pp np vp))
(s -> (np vp))
(s -> (s *conj s))
(start -> (start1))
(start1 -> (dir))
(start1 -> (np))
(start1 -> (s))
(vc -> (*aux *v))
(vc -> (*v))
(vp -> (vc np))
(vp -> (vp *conj vp))
(vp -> (vc)))
```

## Grammar III

```
((ADD -> (VP=EN-NP))
 (ADD -> (*BECAUSE *OF NP))
 (ADD -> (*INSADV))
 (ADD -> (CONJ))
 (ADD -> (PP))
 (ADD -> (*DUE *TO NP))
 (ADD -> (VP=ING))
 (ADJP -> (ADVP *ADJ))
 (ADJP -> (*ADJ))
 (ADJP -> (ADVP *NUMBER))
 (ADJP -> (*NUMBER))
 (ADVP -> (*ADV *ADV))
 (ADVP -> (*ADV))
 (COMP -> (NP))
 (COMP -> (VP=ING))
 (COMP -> (POSTADJP))
 (COMP -> (*THAT SDEC))
 (COMP -> (VP=EN))
 (COMP -> (QNP SDEC-NP))
 (COMP -> (QADV TOINF))
 (COMP -> (QADV SDEC))
 (COMP -> (QNP TOINF-NP))
 (COMP-NP -> (VP=EN-NP))
```

```
(COMP-NP -> (VP=ING-NP))
(COMP-NP -> (NP-NP))
(IMP -> (*PLEASE VP=INF))
(IMP -> (VP=INF))
(IMP -> (VP=INF *COMMA *PLEASE VP=INF))
(IMP -> (VP=INF *PLEASE VP=INF))
(IMP -> (*COULD *YOU *PLEASE VP=INF))
(NM -> (*N *N *N *N))
(NM -> (*N *N *N))
(NM -> (*N))
(NM -> (*N *N))
(NP -> (NP1 POSTADJP))
(NP -> (NP1 RELC))
(NP -> (NP1))
(NP -> (*PRON))
(NP -> (NP1 VP=EN-NP RELC))
(NP -> (T-HERE))
(NP -> (NP1 VP=EN-NP))
(NP -> (NP1 POSTADJP RELC))
(NP -> (*QUANT))
(NP-NP -> NIL)
(NP0 -> (ADJP NP0))
(NP0 -> (NM))
(NP0 -> (*NUMBER))
(NP1 -> (NP1 PP))
(NP1 -> (*DET NP0))
(NP1 -> (NP0))
(NP1 -> (*QUANT))
(POSTADJP -> (*SO ADJP *THAT SDEC))
(POSTADJP -> (ADJP *FOR NP TOINF))
(POSTADJP -> (ADJP TOINF))
(POSTADJP -> (ADJP *FOR NP))
(POSTADJP -> (ADJP))
(PP -> (*PREP NP))
(PP -> (*PREP VP=ING))
(PP-NP -> (*PREP VP=ING-NP))
(PP-NP -> (*PREP NP-NP))
(QADJ -> (*HOW *ADJ))
(QADJ -> (*WHOSE))
(QADV -> (*WHERE))
(QADV -> (*WHEN))
(QADV -> (*HOW))
(QADV -> (*PREP QNP))
(QADV -> (*HOW *ADV))
(QNP -> (*WHOM))
(QNP -> (*WHAT NP))
(QNP -> (*WHICH NP))
(QNP -> (*HOW *QUANT NP))
(QNP -> (*HOW *QUANT))
(QNP -> (*WHOSE NP))
(QNP -> (*WHO))
```

```
(QNP -> (*WHICH))
(QNP -> (*WHAT))
(RELC -> (*PREP RELNP SDEC))
(RELC -> (*WHERE SDEC))
(RELC -> (RELNP SDEC-NP))
(RELC -> (*WHEN SDEC))
(RELC -> (*SUCH *THAT SDEC))
(RELNP -> (*THAT))
(RELNP -> (*WHAT))
(RELNP -> (*WHICH))
(RELNP -> (*WHO))
(RELNP -> (*WHOM))
(RELNP -> (NP *OF RELNP))
(RELNP -> (*WHOSE NP))
(S -> (S *COMMA *CONJ S))
(S -> (*CONJ S *COMMA S))
(S -> (SDEC))
(S -> (WHQ))
(S -> (S *CONJ S))
(S -> (S *COMMA ADD))
(S -> (YNQ))
(S -> (ADD *COMMA S))
(S -> (IMP))
(SDEC -> (SUBJ VP=TENSE))
(SDEC -> (SUBJ *MODAL VP=INF))
(SDEC-NP -> (NP-NP VP=TENSE))
(SDEC-NP -> (SUBJ VP=TENSE-NP))
(SDEC-NP -> (NP-NP *MODAL VP=INF))
(SDEC-NP -> (SUBJ *MODAL VP=INF-NP))
(START -> (S))
(SUBJ -> (*THAT SDEC))
(SUBJ -> (NP))
(SUBJ -> (VP=ING))
(SUBJ -> (TOINF))
(T-HERE -> (*HERE))
(T-HERE -> (*THERE))
(TOINF -> (*TO VP=INF))
(TOINF-NP -> (*TO VP=INF-NP))
(VP=EN -> (VP=EN ADVP))
(VP=EN -> (*BE=EN COMP))
(VP=EN -> (ADVP VP=EN))
(VP=EN -> (VP=EN PP))
(VP=EN -> (VP=EN TOINF))
(VP=EN -> (*NOT VP=EN))
(VP=EN -> (*V=EN))
(VP=EN -> (*V=EN COMP))
(VP=EN -> (*VA=EN NP COMP))
(VP=EN -> (*VB=EN NP VP=INF))
(VP=EN -> (*HAVE=EN VP=EN))
(VP=EN-NP -> (VP=EN-NP ADVP))
(VP=EN-NP -> (*V=EN COMP-NP))
```

```
/P=EN-NP -> (*VA=EN NP-NP COMP))
/P=EN-NP -> (*VA=EN NP COMP-NP))
/P=EN-NP -> (*VB=EN NP-NP VP=INF))
/P=EN-NP -> (*VB=EN NP VP=INF-NP))
/P=EN-NP -> (*BE=EN COMP-NP))
/P=EN-NP -> (*HAVE=EN VP=EN-NP))
/P=EN-NP -> (ADVP VP=EN-NP))
/P=EN-NP -> (VP=EN-NP TOINF))
/P=EN-NP -> (VP=EN TOINF-NP))
/P=EN-NP -> (VP=EN-NP PP))
/P=EN-NP -> (VP=EN PP-NP))
/P=EN-NP -> (*NOT VP=EN-NP))
/P=INF -> (VP=INF TOINF))
/P=INF -> (VP=INF ADVP))
/P=INF -> (*V=INF))
/P=INF -> (*V=INF COMP))
/P=INF -> (ADVP VP=INF))
/P=INF -> (VP=INF PP))
/P=INF -> (*NOT VP=INF))
/P=INF -> (*HAVE=INF VP=EN))
/P=INF -> (*BE=INF COMP))
/P=INF -> (*VA=INF NP COMP))
/P=INF -> (*VB=INF NP VP=INF))
/P=INF-NP -> (VP=INF-NP TOINF))
/P=INF-NP -> (*V=INF COMP-NP))
/P=INF-NP -> (*VA=INF NP-NP COMP))
/P=INF-NP -> (*VA=INF NP COMP-NP))
/P=INF-NP -> (*VB=INF NP-NP VP=INF))
/P=INF-NP -> (*VB=INF NP VP=INF-NP))
/P=INF-NP -> (*BE=INF COMP-NP))
/P=INF-NP -> (*HAVE=INF VP=EN-NP))
/P=INF-NP -> (VP=INF TOINF-NP))
/P=INF-NP -> (*NOT VP=INF-NP))
/P=INF-NP -> (VP=INF-NP ADVP))
/P=INF-NP -> (ADVP VP=INF-NP))
/P=INF-NP -> (VP=INF-NP PP))
/P=INF-NP -> (VP=INF PP-NP))
/P=ING -> (*NOT VP=ING))
/P=ING -> (*VA=ING NP COMP))
/P=ING -> (*HAVE=ING VP=EN))
/P=ING -> (*VB=ING NP VP=INF))
/P=ING -> (*V=ING))
/P=ING -> (*V=ING COMP))
/P=ING -> (*BE=ING COMP))
/P=ING -> (VP=ING PP))
/P=ING -> (ADVP VP=ING))
/P=ING -> (VP=ING ADVP))
/P=ING -> (VP=ING TOINF))
/P=ING-NP -> (*NOT VP=ING-NP))
/P=ING-NP -> (*HAVE=ING VP=EN-NP))
/P=ING-NP -> (*BE=ING COMP-NP))
```

```
(VP=ING-NP -> (*VB=ING NP VP=INF-NP))
(VP=ING-NP -> (*VA=ING NP-NP COMP))
(VP=ING-NP -> (*VA=ING NP COMP-NP))
(VP=ING-NP -> (ADVP VP=ING-NP))
(VP=ING-NP -> (*VB=ING NP-NP VP=INF))
(VP=ING-NP -> (VP=ING-NP TOINF))
(VP=ING-NP -> (VP=ING TOINF-NP))
(VP=ING-NP -> (VP=ING-NP PP))
(VP=ING-NP -> (VP=ING PP-NP))
(VP=ING-NP -> (*V=ING COMP-NP))
(VP=ING-NP -> (VP=ING-NP ADVP))
(VP=TENSE -> (*V=TENSE))
(VP=TENSE -> (*V=TENSE COMP))
(VP=TENSE -> (*VA=TENSE NP COMP))
(VP=TENSE -> (*VB=TENSE NP VP=INF))
(VP=TENSE -> (VP=TENSE ADVP))
(VP=TENSE -> (*HAVE=TENSE VP=EN))
(VP=TENSE -> (*BE=TENSE COMP))
(VP=TENSE -> (*NOT VP=TENSE))
(VP=TENSE -> (VP=TENSE TOINF))
(VP=TENSE -> (VP=TENSE PP))
(VP=TENSE -> (ADVP VP=TENSE))
(VP=TENSE-NP -> (VP=TENSE-NP ADVP))
(VP=TENSE-NP -> (*VA=TENSE NP-NP COMP))
(VP=TENSE-NP -> (*VA=TENSE NP COMP-NP))
(VP=TENSE-NP -> (*V=TENSE COMP-NP))
(VP=TENSE-NP -> (*VB=TENSE NP-NP VP=INF))
(VP=TENSE-NP -> (*VB=TENSE NP VP=INF-NP))
(VP=TENSE-NP -> (*BE=TENSE COMP-NP))
(VP=TENSE-NP -> (*HAVE=TENSE VP=EN-NP))
(VP=TENSE-NP -> (ADVP VP=TENSE-NP))
(VP=TENSE-NP -> (VP=TENSE-NP TOINF))
(VP=TENSE-NP -> (VP=TENSE TOINF-NP))
(VP=TENSE-NP -> (VP=TENSE-NP PP))
(VP=TENSE-NP -> (VP=TENSE PP-NP))
(VP=TENSE-NP -> (*NOT VP=TENSE-NP))
(WHQ -> (QNP YNQ-NP))
(WHQ -> (QADV YNQ))
(WHQ -> (QADJ *BE=TENSE SUBJ))
(YNQ -> (*BE=TENSE SUBJ COMP))
(YNQ -> (*MODAL SUBJ VP=INF))
(YNQ -> (*HAVE=TENSE SUBJ VP=EN))
(YNQ-NP -> (*BE=TENSE SUBJ COMP-NP))
(YNQ-NP -> (*BE=TENSE COMP))
(YNQ-NP -> (*HAVE=TENSE VP=EN))
(YNQ-NP -> (*HAVE=TENSE SUBJ VP=EN-NP))
(YNQ-NP -> (*MODAL VP=INF))
(YNQ-NP -> (*MODAL SUBJ VP=INF-NP))))
```

# Grammar IV

```
((ADJCOMP -> (*RELPRO SDEC))
 (ADJCOMP -> (*P NP INFINITIVE))
 (ADJCOMP -> (*ENOUGH *P NP INFINITIVE))
 (ADJCOMP -> (*ENOUGH *P NP))
 (ADJCOMP -> (*ENOUGH INFINITIVE))
 (ADJCOMP -> (*ENOUGH))
 (ADJCOMP -> (*P NP))
 (ADJCOMP -> (INFINITIVE))
 (ADJP -> (ADJP THANCOMP))
 (ADJP -> (*ADV ADJP))
 (ADJP -> (DETQ *A ADJP))
 (ADJP -> (DETQ *A *Q ADJP))
 (ADJP -> (DETQ ADJP))
 (ADJP -> (*NOT *AS ADJP ASCOMP))
 (ADJP -> (*NOT *SO ADJP ASCOMP))
 (ADJP -> (*Q *ADJ))
 (ADJP -> (ADJP *PARACONJ ADJP))
 (ADJP -> (*AS ADJP))
 (ADJP -> (DETQ *Q ADJP))
 (ADJP -> (*ADJ))
 (ADJP -> (*ADJ ADJCOMP))
 (ADJP -> (*QDET *ADJ))
 (ADJP -> (QPP *QDET *ADJ))
 (ADJP -> (*A *Q ADJP))
 (ADJP -> (DDET *ADJ))
 (ADJP -> (*Q ADJP))
 (ADJP -> (*A ADJP))
 (ADVP -> (DETQ *ADV))
 (ADVP -> (ADVP THANCOMP))
 (ADVP -> (QPP *QDET *ADV))
 (ADVP -> (*Q *ADV))
 (ADVP -> (DETQ *Q *ADV))
 (ADVP -> (*AS ADVP))
 (ADVP -> (*Q *ADV))
 (ADVP -> (*P SDEC))
 (ADVP -> (*SUBCONJ SDEC))
 (ADVP -> (*SUBCONJ VP))
 (ADVP -> (*QDET *ADV))
 (ADVP -> (*ADV))
 (ASCOMP -> (*AS SUBJ BEP))
 (ASCOMP -> (*AS SUBJ AUXD VP2))
 (ASCOMP -> (*AS SUBJ VP2))
 (ASCOMP -> (*AS SDEC))
 (ASCOMP -> (*AS NP))
 (ASCOMP -> (*AS SUBJ AUX BEP))
 (AUX -> (MODALP HAVEP))
 (AUX -> (MODALP BEP))
 (AUX -> (BEP))
```

```
(AUX -> (MODALP))
(AUX -> (HAVEP))
(AUX -> (MODALP HAVEP BEP))
(AUX -> (HAVEP BEP))
(AUXD -> (AUX))
(AUXD -> (DOP))
(BEP -> (*BE))
(BEP -> (*BE *NOT))
(DDET -> (*ALL *NUMBER))
(DDET -> (*ALL QPP))
(DDET -> (*NOT *ALL *NUMBER))
(DDET -> (*NOT *ALL QPP))
(DDET -> (*NOT *ALL *DET QPP))
(DDET -> (*ALL *DET *NUMBER))
(DDET -> (*ALL *DET QPP))
(DDET -> (*NOT *ALL *DET *NUMBER))
(DDET -> (*NOT *ALL))
(DDET -> (*DET QPP))
(DDET -> (*ALL))
(DDET -> (*ALL *DET))
(DDET -> (*DET))
(DDET -> (*NOT *ALL *DET))
(DDET -> (*DET *NUMBER))
(DETQ -> (*NUMBER))
(DETQ -> (*A *NUMBER))
(DETQ -> (DDET *Q))
(DETQ -> (*DET *Q))
(DETQ -> (QPP))
(DETQ -> (*A *Q))
(DOP -> (*DO))
(DOP -> (*DO *NOT))
(GERUND -> (*HAVE *BE PRED))
(GERUND -> (*NOT *HAVE *BE PRED))
(GERUND -> (*BE PRED))
(GERUND -> (*NOT *HAVE *BE VP))
(GERUND -> (*HAVE *BE VP))
(GERUND -> (*NOT *BE VP))
(GERUND -> (*NOT *BE PRED))
(GERUND -> (*NOT *HAVE VP))
(GERUND -> (*HAVE VP))
(GERUND -> (*NOT VP))
(GERUND -> (VP))
(GERUND -> (*BE VP))
(HAVEP -> (*HAVE))
(HAVEP -> (*HAVE *NOT))
(INFINITIVE -> (*TO BEP BEP PRED))
(INFINITIVE -> (*TO BEP VP))
(INFINITIVE -> (*NOT *TO BEP VP))
(INFINITIVE -> (*NOT *TO *HAVE BEP BEP PRED))
(INFINITIVE -> (*NOT *TO BEP BEP PRED))
(INFINITIVE -> (*TO *HAVE BEP VP))
```

```
(INFINITIVE -> (*NOT *TO *HAVE BEP VP))
(INFINITIVE -> (*TO *HAVE BEP BEP PRED))
(INFINITIVE -> (*NOT *TO *HAVE BEP PRED))
(INFINITIVE -> (*TO VP))
(INFINITIVE -> (*TO *HAVE BEP PRED))
(INFINITIVE -> (*TO BEP PRED))
(INFINITIVE -> (*NOT *TO VP))
(INFINITIVE -> (*NOT *TO BEP PRED))
(INFINITIVE -> (*TO *HAVE VP))
(INFINITIVE -> (*NOT *TO *HAVE VP))
(INFINITIVE1 -> (BEP VP))
(INFINITIVE1 -> (*NOT BEP VP))
(INFINITIVE1 -> (BEP BEP PRED))
(INFINITIVE1 -> (*NOT *HAVE BEP PRED))
(INFINITIVE1 -> (*NOT BEP BEP PRED))
(INFINITIVE1 -> (*NOT *HAVE BEP VP))
(INFINITIVE1 -> (*HAVE BEP BEP PRED))
(INFINITIVE1 -> (*HAVE BEP VP))
(INFINITIVE1 -> (VP))
(INFINITIVE1 -> (*NOT VP))
(INFINITIVE1 -> (BEP PRED))
(INFINITIVE1 -> (*NOT *HAVE VP))
(INFINITIVE1 -> (*NOT BEP PRED))
(INFINITIVE1 -> (*HAVE VP))
(INFINITIVE1 -> (*HAVE BEP PRED))
(INFINITREL -> (*P *RELPRO *BE VP))
(INFINITREL -> (*P *RELPRO VP))
(INFINITREL -> (*P *RELPRO INFINITIVE))
(INFINITREL -> (*P NP *BE VP))
(INFINITREL -> (*P NP VP))
(INFINITREL -> (*BE VP))
(INFINITREL -> (*P NP INFINITIVE))
(INFINITREL -> (VP))
(INFINITREL -> (INFINITIVE))
(MODALP -> (*MODAL))
(MODALP -> (*MODAL *NOT))
(NCOMP -> (ADJP))
(NCOMP -> (SREL))
(NCOMP -> (THANCOMP))
(NCOMP -> (NCOMP PP))
(NCOMP -> (INFINITREL))
(NCOMP -> (VP2))
(NCOMP -> (PP))
(NOMHD -> (QPP ADJP NOMHD))
(NOMHD -> (*V NOMHD))
(NOMHD -> (ADJP NOMHD))
(NOMHD -> (*N))
(NOMHD -> (*N *N))
(NOMHD -> (*N *N *N))
(NP -> (DDET *Q ADJP NCOMP))
(NP -> (*DET GERUND))
```

```
(NP -> (GERUND))
(NP -> (*AS QPP))
(NP -> (*AS QPP NOMHD))
(NP -> (*AS *ADJ NP))
(NP -> (*AS QPP NP))
(NP -> (*AS *ADJ NP THANCOMP))
(NP -> (*AS QPP *ADJ NP THANCOMP))
(NP -> (*RELPRO SDEC))
(NP -> (NP *PARACONJ NP))
(NP -> (NP *COMMA NP))
(NP -> (*PRON))
(NP -> (NOMHD))
(NP -> (DDET *Q ADJP NOMHD))
(NP -> (DDET NOMHD))
(NP -> (DETQ NOMHD))
(NP -> (*A NCOMP))
(NP -> (*A NOMHD))
(NP -> (DETQ))
(NP -> (DDET ADJP NP NCOMP))
(NP -> (DDET ADJP NOMHD))
(NP -> (DETQ *Q))
(NP -> (*PRON NCOMP))
(NP -> (NP PP))
(OBJ -> (NP))
(OBJ1 -> (NP))
(OBJ2 -> (NP))
(PP -> (*P NP *PARACONJ NP))
(PP -> (*P OBJ))
(PRED -> (VP2))
(PRED -> (PRED INFINITIVE))
(PRED -> (PRED PP))
(PRED -> (PP))
(PRED -> (NP))
(PRED -> (ADJP))
(QPP -> (*Q QPP))
(QPP -> (*QDET *Q QPP))
(QPP -> (*Q))
(QPP -> (*QDET *Q))
(SCMP -> (VP1 *PARACONJ VP1))
(SCMP -> (VP1 *PARACONJ SDEC))
(SCMP -> (SDEC *COMMA SCMP))
(SCMP -> (SDEC *PARACONJ VP1))
(SCMP -> (SDEC *PARACONJ SDEC))
(SCMP -> (VP1 *COMMA SCMP))
(SDEC -> (SDEC ADVP))
(SDEC -> (SDEC *COMMA VP3))
(SDEC -> (VP3 *COMMA SDEC))
(SDEC -> (*THERE AUX BEP SUBJ PRED))
(SDEC -> (*THERE BEP SUBJ PRED))
(SDEC -> (SDEC *COMMA INFINITIVE))
(SDEC -> (*THERE AUX BEP SUBJ))
```

```
(SDEC -> (SUBJ VP))
(SDEC -> (SUBJ AUXD VP))
(SDEC -> (SUBJ BEP PRED))
(SDEC -> (*THERE BEP SUBJ))
(SDEC -> (SUBJ *BE))
(SDEC -> (SUBJ AUX *BE))
(SDEC -> (SUBJ AUX BEP PRED))
(SENTENCE -> (ADVP *COMMA SENTENCE))
(SENTENCE -> (SIMP *PARACONJ SDEC))
(SENTENCE -> (SIMP *CONJ SDEC))
(SENTENCE -> (SIMP *CONJ SIMP))
(SENTENCE -> (PP *COMMA SENTENCE))
(SENTENCE -> (SWHQ))
(SENTENCE -> (SQ))
(SENTENCE -> (*CONJ SENTENCE))
(SENTENCE -> (SIMP *PARACONJ SIMP))
(SENTENCE -> (SDEC))
(SENTENCE -> (SDEC *COMMA SCMP))
(SENTENCE -> (SIMP *PARACONJ VP1))
(SENTENCE -> (SDEC *CONJ SDEC))
(SENTENCE -> (SDEC *PARACONJ SDEC))
(SENTENCE -> (SDEC *PARACONJ VP1))
(SENTENCE -> (SIMP))
(SENTENCE -> (SIMP *COMMA SCMP))
(SIMP -> (*BE PRED))
(SIMP -> (DOP *BE PRED))
(SIMP -> (SIMP ADVP))
(SIMP -> (VP))
(SIMP -> (DOP VP))
(SQ -> (BEP *THERE SUBJ))
(SQ -> (SQ ADVP))
(SQ -> (BEP *THERE SUBJ PRED))
(SQ -> (MODALP *THERE BEP SUBJ))
(SQ -> (MODALP *THERE BEP SUBJ PRED))
(SQ -> (MODALP *THERE *NOT BEP SUBJ))
(SQ -> (HAVEP *THERE BEP SUBJ PRED))
(SQ -> (MODALP *THERE *NOT BEP SUBJ PRED))
(SQ -> (MODALP *THERE HAVEP BEP SUBJ))
(SQ -> (MODALP *THERE HAVEP BEP SUBJ PRED))
(SQ -> (MODALP *THERE *NOT HAVEP BEP SUBJ))
(SQ -> (MODALP *THERE *NOT HAVEP BEP SUBJ PRED))
(SQ -> (HAVEP *THERE BEP SUBJ))
(SQ -> (HAVEP SUBJ BEP VP))
(SQ -> (BEP SUBJ *NOT VP))
(SQ -> (BEP SUBJ PRED))
(SQ -> (BEP SUBJ *BE PRED))
(SQ -> (MODALP SUBJ BEP PRED))
(SQ -> (MODALP SUBJ HAVEP BEP PRED))
(SQ -> (HAVEP SUBJ *BE PRED))
(SQ -> (DOP SUBJ VP))
(SQ -> (MODALP SUBJ HAVEP BEP VP))
```

```
(SQ -> (MODALP SUBJ VP))
(SQ -> (MODALP SUBJ BEP VP))
(SQ -> (MODALP SUBJ HAVEP VP))
(SQ -> (HAVEP SUBJ VP))
(SQ -> (BEP SUBJ VP))
(SQ1 -> (BEP SUBJ VP2))
(SQ1 -> (BEP SUBJ *NOT VP2))
(SQ1 -> (BEP SUBJ))
(SQ1 -> (MODALP SUBJ HAVEP BEP))
(SQ1 -> (MODALP SUBJ BEP))
(SQ1 -> (HAVEP SUBJ *BE))
(SQ1 -> (SQ1 ADVP))
(SQ1 -> (MODALP SUBJ BEP VP2))
(SQ1 -> (DOP SUBJ VP2))
(SQ1 -> (MODALP SUBJ VP2))
(SQ1 -> (MODALP SUBJ HAVEP VP2))
(SQ1 -> (HAVEP SUBJ BEP VP2))
(SQ1 -> (MODALP SUBJ HAVEP BEP VP2))
(SQ1 -> (HAVEP SUBJ VP2))
(SQ2 -> (MODALP *THERE *NOT HAVEP BEP VP))
(SQ2 -> (MODALP *THERE *NOT HAVEP BEP))
(SQ2 -> (SQ2 ADVP))
(SQ2 -> (MODALP *THERE HAVEP BEP SREL))
(SQ2 -> (MODALP *THERE HAVEP BEP PRED))
(SQ2 -> (MODALP *THERE HAVEP BEP *BE PRED))
(SQ2 -> (MODALP *THERE HAVEP BEP VP))
(SQ2 -> (HAVEP *THERE BEP SREL))
(SQ2 -> (MODALP *THERE *NOT HAVEP BEP *BE PRED))
(SQ2 -> (MODALP *THERE *NOT HAVEP BEP PRED))
(SQ2 -> (MODALP *THERE *NOT HAVEP BEP SREL))
(SQ2 -> (HAVEP *THERE BEP))
(SQ2 -> (HAVEP *THERE BEP VP))
(SQ2 -> (HAVEP *THERE BEP *BE PRED))
(SQ2 -> (HAVEP *THERE BEP PRED))
(SQ2 -> (MODALP *THERE *NOT BEP SREL))
(SQ2 -> (BEP *THERE))
(SQ2 -> (BEP *THERE VP))
(SQ2 -> (BEP *THERE *BE PRED))
(SQ2 -> (BEP *THERE PRED))
(SQ2 -> (BEP *THERE SREL))
(SQ2 -> (MODALP *THERE BEP))
(SQ2 -> (MODALP *THERE BEP VP))
(SQ2 -> (MODALP *THERE *NOT BEP VP))
(SQ2 -> (MODALP *THERE *NOT BEP PRED))
(SQ2 -> (MODALP *THERE *NOT BEP *BE PRED))
(SQ2 -> (MODALP *THERE HAVEP BEP))
(SQ2 -> (MODALP *THERE BEP *BE PRED))
(SQ2 -> (MODALP *THERE BEP SREL))
(SQ2 -> (MODALP *THERE BEP PRED))
(SQ2 -> (MODALP *THERE *NOT BEP))
(SREL -> (*P *RELPRO SDEC))
```

```
(SREL -> (*RELPRO SUBJ VP2))
(SREL -> (*RELPRO SUBJ AUXD VP2))
(SREL -> (*RELPRO SUBJ AUX BEP))
(SREL -> (*RELPRO SUBJ BEP))
(SREL -> (SREL PP))
(SREL -> (*COMMA SREL))
(SREL -> (*RELPRO AUXD VP))
(SREL -> (*RELPRO VP))
(SREL -> (*RELPRO AUX BEP PRED))
(SREL -> (*RELPRO BEP PRED))
(SREL -> (SUBJ AUX BEP))
(SREL -> (SUBJ AUXD VP2))
(SREL -> (SUBJ BEP))
(SREL -> (SUBJ VP2))
(START -> (SENTENCE))
(SUBJ -> (NP))
(SWHQ -> (WHNP AUX BEP))
(SWHQ -> (WHNP VP))
(SWHQ -> (WHNP AUXD VP))
(SWHQ -> (WHNP BEP))
(SWHQ -> (WHADJP SQ))
(SWHQ -> (WHADJP SQ1))
(SWHQ -> (WHPP SQ))
(SWHQ -> (WHNP SQ1))
(SWHQ -> (WHNP SQ2))
(THANCOMP -> (*THAN SUBJ AUX BEP))
(THANCOMP -> (*THAN SUBJ BEP))
(THANCOMP -> (*THAN SUBJ AUXD VP2))
(THANCOMP -> (*THAN SUBJ VP2))
(THANCOMP -> (*THAN NP))
(THANCOMP -> (*THAN SDEC))
(VP -> (*V OBJ ADJP))
(VP -> (*V WHADJP INFINITIVE))
(VP -> (*V WHADJP SDEC))
(VP -> (*V WHNP INFINITIVE))
(VP -> (*V *RELPRO SDEC))
(VP -> (*V WHNP SDEC))
(VP -> (*V WHPP INFINITIVE))
(VP -> (*V WHPP SDEC))
(VP -> (VP PP))
(VP -> (*V OBJ VP))
(VP -> (*V ADVP OBJ))
(VP -> (*V OBJ ADVP))
(VP -> (*V OBJ *BE PRED))
(VP -> (VP INFINITIVE))
(VP -> (VP ADVP))
(VP -> (VP *PARACONJ INFINITIVE))
(VP -> (VP *PARACONJ ADJP))
(VP -> (*V))
(VP -> (*V ADVP))
(VP -> (*V ADJP))
```

```
(VP -> (*V INFINITIVE))
(VP -> (*V VP))
(VP -> (*V *BE PRED))
(VP -> (*V OBJ))
(VP -> (*V *REFL))
(VP -> (*V OBJ INFINITIVE1))
(VP -> (*V OBJ INFINITIVE))
(VP -> (*V INFINITIVE))
(VP -> (*V SDEC))
(VP -> (*V OBJ1 OBJ2))
(VP1 -> (BEP PRED))
(VP1 -> (VP))
(VP2 -> (VP2 ADVP))
(VP2 -> (*V ADJP))
(VP2 -> (VP2 PP))
(VP2 -> (*V *P OBJ1))
(VP2 -> (*V OBJ1))
(VP2 -> (*V INFINITIVE1))
(VP2 -> (*V))
(VP2 -> (*V INFINITIVE))
(VP2 -> (*V ADVP))
(VP3 -> (VP))
(VP3 -> (*HAVE VP))
(VP3 -> (*BE PRED))
(VP3 -> (*HAVE *BE PRED))
(VP3 -> (PRED))
(VP3 -> (*NOT VP3))
(WHADJP -> (*HOW *Q))
(WHADJP -> (*HOW))
(WHADJP -> (*HOW ADJP))
(WHDET -> (*WHN))
(WHDET -> (*HOW *Q))
(WHNP -> (WHDET *NUMBER NCOMP))
(WHNP -> (WHDET *NUMBER))
(WHNP -> (WHDET NOMHD NCOMP))
(WHNP -> (WHDET NCOMP))
(WHNP -> (WHDET NOMHD))
(WHNP -> (WHDET))
(WHPP -> (*WHP))
(WHPP -> (*P *WHP))))
```

# Appendix G
# Sentences Used in the Experiments

Sentence set I is listed here. A brief description of the sample sentences can be found in subsection 6.1.3.

The assembly language provides a means for writing a program without having to be concerned with actual memory addresses. (*det) (*n) (*n) (*v=tense) (*det) (*n *v=inf *v=tense) (*prep) (*v=ing) (*det) (*n *v=inf *v=tense) (*prep) (*have=ing *v=ing *va=ing *vb=ing) (*to *prep) (*be=inf) (*v=en *v=tense) (*prep) (*adj) (*n) (*n *v=tense)

It allows the use of symbolic codes to represent the instructions. (*pron) (*v=tense) (*det) (*n *v=inf *v=tense) (*prep) (*adj) (*n *v=tense) (*to *prep) (*v=inf *v=tense) (*det) (*n)

Labels can be assigned to a particular instruction step in a source program to identify that step as an entry point for use in subsequent instructions. (*n *v=tense) (*modal) (*be=inf) (*v=en *v=tense) (*to *prep) (*det) (*adj) (*n) (*n) (*prep) (*det) (*n) (*n *v=inf *v=tense) (*to *prep) (*v=tense *v=inf) (*that *det *pron) (*n) (*prep *as) (*det) (*n) (*n *v=inf *v=tense) (*prep) (*n *v=inf *v=tense) (*prep) (*adj) (*n)

Operands which follows each instruction represent storage locations. (*n) (*which) (*v=tense) (*det) (*n)·(*v=inf *v=tense) (*n) (*n)

The assembly language also includes assembler directives that supplement the machine instruction. (*det) (*n) (*n) (*adv) (*v=tense) (*n) (*n) (*that *det *pron) (*n *v=inf *v=tense) (*det) (*n) (*n)

A pseudo-op is a statement which is not translated into a machine instruction. (*det) (*n) (*be=tense) (*det) (*n) (*which) (*be=tense) (*not) (*v=tense *v=en) (*prep) (*det) (*n) (*n)

A program written in assembly language is called a source program. (*det) (*n *v=inf *v=tense) (*v=en) (*prep) (*n) (*n) (*be=tense) (*v=en *v=tense *va=en *va=tense) (*det) (*n) (*n *v=inf *v=tense)

It consists of symbolic commands called statements. (*pron) (*v=tense) (*prep) (*adj) (*n) (*v=tense *v=en *va=tense *va=en) (*n)

Each statement is written on a single line, and it may consist of four entries. (*det) (*n) (*be=tense) (*v=en) (*prep) (*det) (*adj) (*n *v=inf *v=tense)

**185**

(*comma) (*conj) (*pron) (*modal) (*v=inf *v=tense) (*prep) (*number) (*n)

The source program is processed by the assembler to obtain a machine language program that can be executed directly by the CPU. (*det) (*n) (*n *v=inf *v=tense) (*be=tense) (*v=tense *v=en) (*prep) (*det) (*n) (*to *prep) (*v=inf *v=tense) (*det) (*n) (*n) (*n *v=inf *v=tense) (*that *det *pron) (*modal) (*be=inf) (*v=tense *v=en) (*adv) (*prep) (*det) (*n)

Ethernet is a broadcast communication system for carrying digital data packets among computing stations which are locally distributed. (*n) (*be=tense) (*det) (*v=tense *v=inf *v=en *n) (*n) (*n) (*prep) (*v=ing) (*adj) (*n) (*n) (*prep) (*adj) (*n) (*which) (*be=tense) (*adv) (*v=tense *v=en)

The packet transport mechanism provided by Ethernet has been used to build systems which can be local computer networks. (*det) (*n) (*n) (*n) (*v=en *v=tense *va=en *va=tense) (*prep) (*n) (*have=tense *v=tense *va=tense *vb=tense) (*be=en) (*v=tense *v=en) (*to *prep) (*v=inf *v=tense) (*n) (*which) (*modal) (*be=inf) (*adj) (*n) (*n)

Switching of packets to their destinations on the Ether is distributed among the receiving stations using packet address recognition. (*v=ing) (*prep) (*n) (*to *prep) (*det) (*n) (*prep) (*det) (*n) (*be=tense) (*v=tense *v=en) (*prep) (*det) (*adj) (*n) (*prep) (*n) (*n *v=inf *v=tense) (*n)

A model for estimating performance under heavy loads is included for completeness. (*det) (*n *v=inf *v=tense) (*prep) (*v=ing) (*n) (*prep) (*adj) (*n) (*be=tense) (*v=tense *v=en) (*prep) (*n)

In writing this book, I had several purposes in mind. (*prep) (*v=ing) (*det *pron) (*n) (*comma) (*pron) (*have=tense *have=en *v=tense *v=en *va=tense *va=en *vb=tense *vb=en) (*adj) (*n *v=tense) (*prep) (*n)

It is a text book for students who are beginning graduate work in computer science. (*pron) (*be=tense) (*det) (*n) (*n) (*prep) (*n) (*who) (*be=tense) (*v=ing) (*n *v=inf *v=tense) (*n *v=inf *v=tense) (*prep) (*n) (*n)

It includes exercises designed to help the student master a body of techniques. (*pron) (*v=tense) (*n) (*v=tense *v=en) (*to *prep) (*v=inf *v=tense *vb=inf *vb=tense *n) (*det) (*n) (*n *v=inf *v=tense) (*det) (*n) (*prep) (*n)

It is a practical guide for people who are building computer systems that deal with natural language. (*pron) (*be=tense) (*det) (*adj) (*n) (*prep) (*n) (*who) (*be=tense) (*n *v=ing) (*n) (*n) (*that *det *pron) (*n *v=inf *v=tense) (*prep) (*adj) (*n)

It is not structured as a "how-to" book, but it describes the relevant techniques in detail, and it includes an extensive outline of English grammar. (*pron) (*be=tense) (*not) (*v=tense *v=en) (*prep *as) (*det) (*n) (*n) (*comma) (*conj) (*pron) (*v=tense) (*det) (*adj) (*n) (*prep) (*n) (*comma) (*conj) (*pron) (*v=tense) (*det) (*adj) (*n *v=inf *v=tense) (*prep) (*n *adj) (*n)

It is a reference source with many pointers into the literature of linguistics.
(*pron) (*be=tense) (*det) (*n) (*n) (*prep) (*quant *adj) (*n) (*prep) (*det)
(*n) (*prep) (*n)

I have attempted to introduce a wide variety of material to provide newcomers
with broad access to the field  (*pron) (*have=inf *have=tense *v=inf *v=tense
*va=inf *va=tense *vb=inf *vb=tense) (*v=tense *v=en) (*to *prep) (*v=inf
*v=tense) (*det) (*adj) (*n) (*prep) (*n) (*to *prep) (*v=inf *v=tense) (*n)
(*prep) (*adj) (*n *v=inf *v=tense) (*to *prep) (*det) (*n)

Each chapter includes suggestions for further reading, and there is an
extensive bibliography. (*det) (*n) (*v=tense) (*n) (*prep) (*adj) (*n *v=ing)
(*comma) (*conj) (*there *adv) (*be=tense) (*det) (*adj) (*n)

However, I have tried to limit the references to easily available material.
(*insadv) (*comma) (*pron) (*have=inf *have=tense *v=inf *v=tense *va=inf
*va=tense *vb=inf *vb=tense) (*v=tense *v=en) (*to *prep) (*n *v=inf *v=tense)
(*det) (*n) (*to *prep) (*adv) (*adj) (*n)

This is a book about human language. (*det *pron) (*be=tense) (*det) (*n)
(*prep) (*n) (*n)

Its approach is motivated by two questions. (*det) (*n *v=inf *v=tense)
(*be=tense) (*v=tense *v=en) (*prep) (*number) (*n)

What knowledge must a person have to speak language? (*what) (*n) (*modal)
(*det) (*n) (*have=inf *have=tense *v=inf *v=tense *va=inf *va=tense *vb=inf
*vb=tense) (*to *prep) (*v=inf *v=tense) (*n)

How is the mind organized to make use of this knowledge in communicating?
(*how) (*be=tense) (*det) (*n *v=inf *v=tense) (*v=tense *v=en) (*to *prep)
(*v=tense *v=inf *va=tense *va=inf) (*n *v=inf *v=tense) (*prep) (*det *pron)
(*n) (*prep) (*v=ing)

In looking at language as a cognitive process, we deal with issues that have
been the focus of linguistic study for many years, and this book includes
insights gained from these studies. (*prep) (*v=ing) (*prep) (*n) (*as *prep)
(*det) (*adj) (*n) (*comma) (*pron) (*n *v=inf *v=tense) (*prep) (*n *v=tense)
(*that *det *pron) (*have=inf *have=tense *v=inf *v=tense *va=inf *va=tense
*vb=inf *vb=tense) (*be=en) (*det) (*n *v=inf *v=tense) (*prep) (*adj) (*n
*v=inf *v=tense) (*prep) (*quant *adj) (*n) (*comma) (*conj) (*det *pron) (*n)
(*v=tense) (*n) (*v=tense *v=en) (*prep) (*det *pron) (*n *v=tense)

We look at language from a different perspective. (*pron) (*n *v=inf *v=tense)
(*prep) (*n) (*prep) (*det) (*adj) (*n)

In forty years, since digital computers were developed, people have programmed
them to perform many activities that we think of as requiring some form of
intelligence. (*prep) (*number) (*n) (*comma) (*conj) (*adj) (*n) (*be=tense)
(*v=en *v=tense) (*comma) (*n) (*have=inf *have=tense *v=inf *v=tense *va=inf

*va=tense *vb=inf *vb=tense) (*v=tense *v=en) (*pron) (*to *prep) (*v=inf
*v=tense) (*quant *adj) (*n) (*that *det *pron) (*pron) (*v=inf *v=tense)
(*prep) (*as *prep) (*v=ing) (*det) (*n) (*prep) (*n)

Our study of the mental processes involved in language draws heavily on
concepts that have been developed in the area called artificial intelligence.
(*det) (*n *v=inf *v=tense) (*prep) (*det) (*n *v=tense) (*v=tense *v=en)
(*prep) (*n) (*v=tense) (*adv) (*prep) (*n) (*that *det *pron) (*have=inf
*have=tense *v=inf *v=tense *va=inf *va=tense *vb=inf *vb=tense) (*be=en)
(*v=tense *v=en) (*prep) (*det) (*n) (*v=tense *v=en *va=tense *va=en) (*adj)
(*n)

It is safe to say that much of the work in computer science has been pragmatic,
based on a desire to produce computer programs that can perform useful tasks.
(*pron) (*be=tense) (*adj) (*to *prep) (*v=inf *v=tense) (*that *det *pron)
(*quant *adj) (*prep) (*det) (*n *v=inf *v=tense) (*prep) (*n) (*n)
(*have=tense *v=tense *va=tense *vb=tense) (*be=en) (*adj) (*comma) (*v=tense
*v=en) (*prep) (*det) (*n *v=inf *v=tense) (*to *prep) (*v=inf *v=tense) (*n)
(*n *v=tense) (*that *det *pron) (*modal) (*v=inf *v=tense) (*adj) (*n)

The same concept of program can be applied to the understanding of any system
which is executing processes that can be understood as the rule-governed
manipulation of symbols. (*det) (*adj) (*n) (*prep) (*n *v=inf *v=tense)
(*modal) (*be=inf) (*v=tense *v=en) (*to *prep) (*det) (*n *v=ing) (*prep)
(*det) (*n) (*which) (*be=tense) (*v=ing) (*n *v=tense) (*that *det *pron)
(*modal) (*be=inf) (*v=en) (*as *prep) (*det) (*adj) (*n) (*prep) (*n)

The next chapter sets the computational approach into the context of other
approaches to language by giving a brief history of the major directions in
linguistics. (*det) (*adj) (*n) (*n *v=tense) (*det) (*adj) (*n *v=inf
*v=tense) (*prep) (*det) (*n) (*prep) (*adj) (*n *v=tense) (*to *prep) (*n)
(*prep) (*v=ing *va=ing) (*det) (*adj) (*n) (*prep) (*det) (*n *adj) (*n)
(*prep) (*n)

In performing a mental task like deciding on a chess move, we are aware of
going through a sequence of thought process, as we shall see in later chapters.
(*prep) (*v=ing) (*det) (*adj) (*n) (*v=inf *v=tense *prep) (*v=ing) (*prep)
(*det) (*n) (*n *v=inf *v=tense) (*comma) (*pron) (*be=tense) (*adj) (*prep)
(*v=ing) (*prep) (*det) (*n) (*prep) (*n) (*n *v=tense)

Run. (*v=inf *v=tr se)

Do it. (*v=inf *v=tense *modal) (*pron)

I have a pen. (*pron) (*have=inf *have=tense *v=inf *v=tense *va=inf *va=tense
*vb=inf *vb=tense) (*det) (*n)

I must not do that. (*pron) (*modal) (*not) (*v=inf *v=tense *modal) (*that
*det *pron)

Time flies like an arrow. (*v=inf *v=tense *n) (*v=tense *n) (*v=inf *v=tense *prep) (*det) (*n)

# Appendix H
# Nishida and Doshita's System

---

[14]The prototype of our interactive machine translation system described in chapter 9 is Nishida and Doshita's Machine Translation system [39]. This system translates sentences from English into Japanese in a sentence-by-sentence manner. The main characteristic of this system is in its mechanism for generating the target language sentences. It generates sentences in the same way as sentences are interpreted in Montague semantics [38]. The meaning of each lexical item in the source language is represented as a function which will generate corresponding syntactic and semantic structure of the target language. Once an intermediate representation, a version of an intensional logical form, it is viewed as a target language generation function for the given sentence and is evaluated after substituting for each lexical item.

The main advantage of this system lies in its conceptual simplicity of transfer-generation processing. This system has no big central grammar which might persue arbitrarily complex structural transformation to every details. Instead, what the grammar designer has to do in this system after the analysis grammar is written is just to elaborate a target language generation function for each lexical item. This involves designing for a transitive verb a function which takes two arguments corresponding to the subject and the object and which generates a sentence structure. The system provides a syntactic and semantic projection package for doing this. Linguistic operation such as passivization is represented by a pseudo lexical item (passivizer) to which a function is assigned such that it takes a function for a transitive verb and it will generate a function behaving like a one place function for an intransitive verb. Thus this system is completely lexicon-driven.

The system was implemented in 1982 and a non-trivial grammar was written. It adopted relatively simple parser for analysis. It employed a backtracking mechanism to produce a possible analysis at a time. It asked the user whether the result of the analysis was correct or

---

[14]Appendix H is written by Toyoaki Nishida.

not. The system has been tested against several hundred sentences taken from some scientific or technical literature in computer science. A system with refined and more advanced mechanism was proposed recently [40].

# References

[1]  Aho, A. V. and Ullman, J. D.
     *The Theory of Parsing, Translation and Compiling.*
     Prentice-Hall, Englewood Cliffs, N. J., 1972.

[2]  Aho, A. V. and Johnson, S. C.
     LR parsing.
     *Computing Surveys* 6:2:99-124, 1974.

[3]  Aho, A. V., Johnson, S. C. and Ullman, J. D.
     Deterministic parsing of ambiguous grammars
     *Comm. ACM* 18:8:441-452, 1975.

[4]  Aho, A. V. and Ullman, J. D.
     *Principles of Compiler Design.*
     Addison Wesley, 1977.

[5]  Berwick, R. C. and Weinberg, A. S.
     Parsing Efficiency, Computational Complexity, and the Evaluation of Grammatical
        Theories.
     *Linguistic Inquiry* 13(2):165-192, Spring, 1982.

[6]  Berwick, R. C.
     A Deterministic Parser with Broad Coverage.
     *Proceedings of IJCAI83* :pp.710, August, 1983.

[7]  Birnbaum, L. and Selfridge, M.
     *Conceptual Analysis of Natural Language.*
     Lawrence Erlbaum Associates, Hillsdale, New Jersey, 1981, pages pp.318.

[8]  Bouckaert, M., Pirotte, A. and Snelling, M.
     Efficient Parsing Algorithms for General Context-free Grammars.
     *Inf. Sci.* 8(1):1-26, Jan, 1975.

[9]  Bresnan, J. and Kaplan, R.
     *Lexical-Functional Grammar: A Formal System for Grammatical Representation.*
     MIT Press, Cambridge, Massachusetts, 1982, pages pp. 173-281.

**193**

[10]    Brown, J. S., Burton, R. R. and Kleer, J.
        *Pedagogical, Natural Language and Knowledge Engineering Techniques in SOPHIE
        I, II, and III.*
        Academic Press, London, England, 1982, .

[11]    Carbonell, J. G. and Hayes, P. J.
        *Recovery Strategies for Parsing Extragrammatical Language.*
        Technical Report CMU-CS-84-107, Computer Science Department, Carnegie-Mellon
        University, Feb, 1984.

[12]    Carbonell, J. G.
        Towards a Self-Extending Parser.
        In *Proceedings of 17th Annual Meeting of the Association for Computational
        Linguistics.* August, 1979.

[13]    Carbonell, J. G., Cullingford, R. E. and Gershman, A. V.
        Steps toward Knowledge-Based Machine Translation.
        *IEEE Transactions on Pattern Analysis and Machine Intelligence* PAMI-3(4), July,
        1981.

[14]    Carbonell, J. G. and Tomita, M.
        New Approaches to Machine Translation.
        In *Conference on Theoretical and Methodological Issues in Machine Translation of
        Natural Languages.* Colgate University, August, 1985.
        also available as Tech. Report, Computer Science Department, Carnegie-Mellon
        University, July, 1985.

[15]    Chomsky, N.
        *Aspects of the Theory of Syntax.*
        MIT Press, Cambridge, Mass., 1965.

[16]    Church, K. and Patil, R.
        *Coping with Syntactic Ambiguity or How to Put the Block in the Box on the Table.*
        Technical Report MIT/LCS/TM-216, Lab. for Computer Science, Massachusetts
        Institute of Technology, April, 1982.

[17]    Cocke, J. and Schwartz, J. I.
        *Programming Languages and Their Compilers.*
        Courant Institute of Mathematical Sciences, New York University, New York, 1970.

[18]    Deremer, F. L.
        *Practical Translators for LR(k) Languages.*
        PhD thesis, MIT, 1969.

[19]    DeRemer, F. L.
        Simple LR(k) grammars.
        *Comm. ACM* 14:7:453-460, 1971.

[20] Earley, J.
*An Efficient Context-free Parsing Algorithm.*
PhD thesis, Computer Science Department, Carnegie-Mellon University, 1968.

[21] Earley, J.
An Efficient Context-free Parsing Algorithm.
*Communication of ACM* 6(8):94-102, February, 1970.

[22] Fischer, M. J. and Meyer, A. R.
Boolean Matrix Multiplication and Transitive Closure.
In *IEEE Conf. Rec. Symp. Switching Automata Theory*, pages 129-131. 1971.

[23] Gazdar, G.
*Phrase Structure Grammar.*
D. Reidel, 1982, pages 131-186.

[24] Gazdar, G.
Phrase Structure Grammars and Natural Language.
*Proceedings of IJCAI83* v.1, August, 1983.

[25] Graham, S. L. and Harrison, M. A.
*Parsing of General Context-free Languages.*
Academic Press, New York, 1976, pages 77-185.

[26] Graham, S. L., Harrison, M. A. and Ruzzo, W. L.
An Improved Context-free Recognizer.
*ACM Transactions on Programming Languages and Systems* 2(3):415-462, July, 1980.

[27] Hayes, P. J. and Carbonell, J. G.
*A Tutorial on Techniques and Applications for Natural Language Processing.*
Technical Report CMU-CS-83-158, Computer Science Department, Carnegie-Mellon
       University, October, 1983.

[28] Jacobson, B.
*Transformational-generative Grammar.*
North Holland, Amsterdam, 1978.

[29] Johnson, S. C.
*YACC -- Yet Another Compiler Compiler.*
Technical Report CSTR 32, Bell Laboratories, 1975.

[30] Kaplan, R. M.
*A general syntactic processor.*
Algorithmics Press, New York, 1973, pages 193-241.

[31] Kay, M.
*The MIND System.*
Algorithmics Press, New York, 1973, pages pp.155-188.

[32] Kay, M.
Functional Grammar.
In *Fifth Annual Meeting of the Berkeley Linguistic Society*, pages pp. 142-158.
Berkeley Linguistic Society, MIT Press, Berkeley, California, February, 1979.

[33] Kay, M.
Machine Translation.
*American Journal of Computational Liguistics* vol.8(no.2):pp.74-78, April-June, 1982.

[34] Langendoen, D. T.
Finite-state Parsing of Phrase-Structure Languages and the Status of Readjustment
Rules in Grammar.
*Linguistic Inquiry* 6(4):533-554, fall, 1975.

[35] Hendrix, G. G.
*The LIFER mannual: A Guide to Building Practical Natural Language Interfaces.*
Technical Report TR-138, SRI International, 1977.

[36] Marcus, M. P.
*A Theory of Syntactic Recognition for Natural Language.*
The MIT Press, Cambridge, Massachusetts, 1980.

[37] Matsumoto, Y., Tanaka, H., Hirakawa, H., Miyoshi, H. and Yasukawa, H.
BUP: A Bottom-Up Parser Embedded in Prolog.
*New Generation Computing* 1:pp.145-158, 1983.

[38] Montague, R.
*Universal Grammar.*
Yale University, 1974, pages 222-246.

[39] Nishida, T. and Doshita, S.
Application of Montague Grammar to English-Japanese Machine Translation.
In *Proceedings of Conference on Applied Natural Language Processing*, pages 156-165.
1983.

[40] Nishida, T. and Doshita, S.
Combining Functionality and Object-Orientedness for Natural Language Processing.
In *Proceeings of 10th International Conference on Computational Liguistics
(COLING84)*, pages 218 . July, 1984.

[41] Pereira, F. and Warren, D.
Definite Clause Grammar for Language Analysis.
*Artificial Intelligence* 13:pp.231-278, May, 1980.

[42] Carnegie Group Inc.
PLUME user's manual (unpublished).
1984.

[43]  Pratt, V. R.
      LINGOL -- A Progress Report.
      In *Proc. of 4th IJCAI*, pages pp.327-381. August, 1975.

[44]  Saito, H. and Tomita, M.
      *On Automatic Composition of Stereotypic Documents in Foreign Languages.*
      Technical Report, Computer Science Department, Carnegie-Mellon University, 1985.

[45]  Shank, R. C.
      *Fundamental Studies in Computer Science.* Volume 3: *Conceptual Information Processing.*
      North-Holland Publishing Company, 1975.

[46]  Sheil, B.
      Observations on context-free parsing.
      *Statistical Methods in Linguistics* :71-109, 1976.

[47]  Shieber, S. M.
      Sentence Disambiguation by a Shift-Reduce Parsing Technique.
      *Proceedings of the Eighth International Joint Conference on Artificial Intelligence* v.2, August, 1983.

[48]  Takakura, S.
      A Parser of English in Prolog.
      1984.
      B.S. thesis (in Japanese), Tokyo Institute of Technology.

[49]  Tomita, M.
      LR Parsers For Natural Languages.
      In *Proceeings of 10th International Conference on Computational Liguistics (COLING84).* 1984.

[50]  Tomita, M.
      Disambiguating Grammatically Ambiguous Sentences by Asking.
      In *Proceeings of 10th International Conference on Computational Liguistics (COLING84).* 1984.

[51]  Tomita, M., Nishida, T. and Doshita, S.
      User Front-End for disambiguation in Interactive Machine Translation System.
      In *IPSJ Symposium on Natural Language Processing (in Japanese).* Information Processing Society of Japan, 1984.

[52]  Tomita, M.
      *An Efficient All-Paths Parsing Algorithm for Natural Langauges.*
      Technical Report CMU-CS-84-163, Computer Science Department, Carnegie-Mellon University, Oct., 1984.

[53]   Tomita, M.
       An Efficient Context-free Parsing Algorithm for Natural Lnaguages.
       In *9th International Joint Conference on Artificial Intelligence (IJCAI85)*. August,
       1985.

[54]   Tomita, M.
       Feasibility Study of Personal/Interactive Machine Translation Systems.
       In *Conference on Theoretical and Methodological Issues in Machine Translation of
       Natural Languages*. Colgate University, August, 1985.
       also available as Tech. Report, Computer Science Department, Carnegie-Mellon
       University, July, 1985.

[55]   Valiant, L.
       General Context-free Recognition in Less than Cubic Time.
       *J. Comput Syst. Sci.* 10:308-315, 1975.

[56]   Walters, D. A.
       Deterministic Context-Sensitive Languages.
       *Information and Control* 17:14-40, 1970.

[57]   Winograd, T.
       *Language as a Cognitive Process.*
       Addison-Wesley, 1983.

[58]   Woods, W. A.
       Transition network grammars for natural language analysis.
       *CACM* 13(10):591-606, 1970.

[59]   Younger, D. H.
       Recognition and Parsing of Context-free Languages in time $n^3$.
       *Information and Control* 10(2):189-208, 1967.

# Subject Index

# Author Index